desperate

Hope *for the* Mom
Who Needs to Breathe

SARAH MAE & SALLY CLARKSON

Thomas Nelson
Since 1798

NASHVILLE DALLAS MEXICO CITY RIO DE JANEIRO

Published in Nashville, Tennessee, by Thomas Nelson. Thomas Nelson is a registered trademark of Thomas Nelson, Inc.

Thomas Nelson, Inc., titles may be purchased in bulk for educational, business, fund-raising, or sales promotional use. For information, please e-mail SpecialMarkets@ThomasNelson.com.

Library of Congress Cataloging-in-Publication Data

Mae, Sarah, 1980-
Desperate : hope for the mom who needs to breathe / Sarah Mae and Sally Clarkson.
p. cm.
ISBN 978-1-4002-0466-3
1. Mothers--Religious life. 2. Motherhood--Religious aspects--Christianity. I. Clarkson, Sally. II. Title.
BV4529.18.M34 2013
248.8'431--dc23

2012029682

Printed in the United States of America

16 17 18 RRD 18 17 16 15 14 13

Praise for Desperate

I was surprised by *Desperate.* I didn't expect to laugh, to sigh, to learn and wish I had read this book when I was a young Mom. *Desperate* won't offer you formulas but great ideas, a new perspective, and a deep authentic transparency. You'll feel like Sarah and Sally are your friends on the mom road. Trust me! You need this book! I'm buying it for all my friends who are in the mom stage of life.

—Linda Dillow, author of *Calm My Anxious Heart* and *What's it Like to be Married to Me?*

Sarah Mae and Sally Clarkson are the perfect duo. Through Sarah Mae's transparency, all moms have the chance to exhale. Then as we breathe in Sally's words of wisdom and hope, a healing balm covers the weary mom's heart. Sally and Sarah's compassion for a generation of desperate moms and their faith that drives them to the foot of the cross, will propel women forward as they seek to live the life, God intended for them to live!

—Courtney Joseph, *Women Living Well Ministries*

If ever a mothering book was crafted for me, this is it! Like Sally I have been a mom for a while. I have older kids, each with unique personalities, talents and challenges. Yet like Sarah Mae, I'm also a mom of a busy toddler. This book seeps wisdom and truth. I breathed a sigh of relief to know I'm not alone in my parenting struggles. As a reader I felt part of their friendship circle, and I found hope, answers, and assurance within these pages. I can't recommend this book enough! Read it alone or read it with friends . . . but read it!

—Tricia Goyer, best-selling author of 34 books, including *Blue Like Play Dough: The Shape of Motherhood in the Grip of God*

Sarah Mae represents so many women who long to be good mamas to their little ones, and Sally embodies the mentor so many of us wish we had. They have given us a gift with the words on these pages—a peek into their conversations about what it means to persevere through the tiring days of parenting small children, and a glimpse at what it's like on the other side. *Desperate* is powerful encouragement for young mothers to parent with intention and hope, and for older mothers to prayerfully seek out and mentor a mom just beginning. I am grateful for both of them.

—Tsh Oxenreider, author and blogger behind SimpleMom.net; author and creative director of SimpleLivingMedia.com

With *Desperate*, Sarah Mae and Sally Clarkson touch the tender, innermost depths of a mother's heart. Sarah Mae articulates the struggles that may have remained unspoken in all of us. She is courageous and breathtakingly honest while giving voice to the real challenges of motherhood and the frailty of a woman's soul. Sally Clarkson answers those anguished thoughts with sage, sound, gentle mentoring and the kind friendship of a woman who has walked the same path. Together, they offer today's desperate (or even simply soul-weary) mothers hope, encouragement, and a tangible roadmap for navigating the rough paths along motherhood's journey.

—Elizabeth Foss, author of *Small Steps for Catholic Moms* and *Real Learning: Education in the Heart of the Home*

Powerful, captivating, and gut-wrenchingly honest; if this superb book could get into the hands of every mom, our world would drastically change, for the good! It's a new classic for a new generation.

— Kristen Habermehl, author and speaker from *www.MyHeartAtHome.com*

Vulnerable yet practical, honest yet graceful. The greatest gift within these pages is the encouragement and freedom to mother just as you are.

—Amy Lynn Andrews; author of *Tell Your Time* and AmyLynnAndrews.com

I can't think of a better message for moms to read as we all strive and struggle to be that "perfect" mom. I love how Sally & Sarah Mae share from their hearts, their disappointments, and heartbreaks and offer much needed wisdom, compassion, and understanding. This book is a must read for all moms!

—Angela Perritt, author and co-creator of GoodMorningGirls.org

Nobody places expectations on themselves quite as heavy and overwhelming as mothers. And no one is quite as hard on themselves when they can't live up to their own impossibly high standards. . . . If you're a tired mom who doesn't have time for a day off, this book might be the next best thing. It was for me.

—Lisa-Jo Baker, social media manager for DaySpring, community manager for *incourage.me*, and author of LisaJoBaker.com

Many motherhood books leave me feeling overwhelmed as I struggle to implement their hindsight ideals into my nitty gritty days. *Desperate* is different. Between Sarah Mae's real world "right in the thick of it" honesty and Sally's depth of experience, each chapter both comforts and inspires. It reads like coffee with a compassionate friend and a trusted mentor.

—Kat Lee, author of InspiredToAction.com

Every mom I know has been desperate at some point in her mothering journey, either for a break or a breakthrough. Without a doubt, motherhood is the hardest work I've ever done. *Desperate* reminds mothers they are not alone and offers the beautiful truth that our desperation is the perfect place for His glory.

—Kristen Welch, author of *Don't Make Me Come Up There*

Any mother—whether she is gasping for air or invigorated by her calling—will feel profoundly encouraged by spending time with the honest, wise, and compassionate Sarah Mae & Sally Clarkson in *Desperate: Hope for the Mom Who Needs to Breathe*. Though I wasn't feeling particularly desperate when I read this book, God used it to breathe great life into me, surprising me with newfound courage, inspiring me to draw near to Him, and beckoning me to thrive in my home.

—Laura Booz, mother of three, author of *Blogger Behave*

Every single mom needs to read *Desperate*! Sally and Sarah Mae have hit right at the heart of an epidemic that is sweeping our nation. In our fast-paced culture of today, moms are more exhausted than ever, lacking mentorship, and needing real encouragement . . . and a break. *Desperate* will bring sweet comfort to your soul and inspire you to embrace the role that God has given you like never before.

—Ruth Schwenk, speaker, writer, and
creator of TheBetterMom.com

Desperate is a wonderful balance between two ends of motherhood. Sarah shares raw and detailed emotions about mothering young ones, as she is currently in the heat of it with her three small ones. Sally brings the wisdom from a mother who has been there, and ran the race well, very well. . . . This book isn't only for the desperate moms, it is for ALL moms. Those of us who don't feel quite as desperate can learn (or be reminded of) how vitally important it is to reach out to mothers around us who are struggling. . . .

—Carisa, author of www.iplusiplusiequalsi.net

Sarah Mae and Sally's words are compelling, captivating, and entertaining. Mothers may be knee-deep in dishes and diapers, but they're destined to change the world. The fusion of personal stories, brutal honesty, and biblically-based wisdom make this book a timely gift to a new generation of women. I'm left with renewed vision and deep gratitude.

—Katy Rose; fellow writer at Momheart.com

Expelling the myth that being a mom should be a breeze for every woman who loves her child, *Desperate* examines motherhood with an honest lens. Authors Sarah Mae and Sally peel back layers of unfounded clichés and lofty expectations to send a message of hopefulness to moms of young children. *Desperate* is beautifully and smartly written. It is filled with biblical truth, timely encouragement, and practical examples sure to provide solace to the hearts of all moms who just need to "catch their breath."

—Angela Nazworth, author of AngelaNazworth.com
and writer at incourage.me

. . . Instead of heaping guilt upon moms by giving them impossible-to-live-up-to formulas for perfect parenting, *Desperate* offers a refreshingly-needed message of grace for weary moms. If you've ever struggled with feelings of inadequacy in your mothering, you need to read this book. I guarantee you will be blessed!

—Crystal Paine, Money Saving Mom®

Motherhood is an emotional roller coaster ride. One moment finds you blessed and proud; the next leaves you stressed and drained. The ups and downs wreak havoc on your heart, often knocking the wind right out of your maternal sails. *Desperate* is a mom's manual for what to do—and what not to do—when you feel the ride is just too scary and you don't know how you'll ever hold on. Sarah's honest questions and Sally's seasoned advice, laced with biblical insight and hopeful encouragement, will enable mothers of all ages and stages to find strength amidst the struggles, calm with every climb and peace in every plunge.

—Karen Ehman, Proverbs 31 Ministries director of speakers,
author of six books including *LET. IT. GO.*
How to Stop Running the Show & Start Walking in
Faith, wife of Todd and mother of three

. . . This is by far the best book on mothering I have ever read. It is a must read for every mom who feels they are less than perfect and have been in a place of desperation for help. Help is here.

—Christin Slade, joyfulmothering.net; christinslade.com

This book is a legacy for my children, my grandchildren, my great-grandchildren, and every young woman who needs hope in the precious but weary season of little ones.

Ella, Caedmon, and Caroline, you fill my heart with such joy. My heart overflows with love, admiration, and respect for you. You are beautiful souls. I love you, my darlings, a hundred-thousand-million times and to the Brookshire's and back. Thank you for letting me "keep you."

Sarah Mae

Sarah, Joel, Nathan, and Joy, my precious children,

You are the most profound story that I have ever written, the best work I have ever accomplished—the magnum opus of my life. You are the reason for this message that God has crafted in my soul. May you find His grace filling your days, joy bubbling over at every turn, and love to satisfy the deepest places of your hearts.

You are my treasures.

Sally

Contents

Foreword

And so God orchestrates it that I'm writing these words while sitting in an ER, waiting for chest X-ray results.

For pneumonia.

I am a mama to six, and I've known desperate and wondered how in the world I would find space to breathe.

I remember that day nearly twenty years ago now, when a purple line bled across that strip of paper and I cried. Positive. Pregnant. A person growing within my womb? My hand trembled and my stomach lurched and then I slid to the floor, hugged my knees, and rocked. Cradling me and our firstborn not yet born.

What business did God have giving this twenty-one-year-old a soul to birth? I'd been married less than a dozen weeks. But more critical than being young was the anguishing knowledge of how broken I was, how little I had to offer in the shaping of another human being.

If I was bent and crooked, how could I possibly raise a sapling into a straight, strong tree?

I cried myself to sleep. We told no one in our church family that I was expecting until I was seven months pregnant.

All those years, I tried to stay quiet and hide. Through all the babies who came early and the ones who came breech, through the thirteen years and three months of straight diaper changing and boys who flung toilet bowl plungers to ceilings . . . that then came down and graced a brother with a black eye.

I've been the mama who punished when I needed to pray. Who hollered at kids when I needed to help them. Who lunged onward when I needed to lean on Jesus.

I've lain in bed too scared to get up and ruin another day—ruin my kids.

I wish I had reached out and let someone gently mentor me: How did God Almighty parent His children? What would matter most as I mothered? How could I mother with a heart after God's?

And on a warm day in early June, after I had been a mother for more than a decade, when some of my babies had grown into teens, I sat in Sarah Mae's backyard under the shade of some old branches and pulled her little boy, Caed, up on my lap. He turned the pages of a picture book, and I made the sounds of the jungle animals and he covered his mouth when he giggled. Caroline and Ella ran in and out of a playhouse. And Sarah Mae and I sat together as two mothers with two daughters, longing to leave a legacy for our daughters to be mothers after our Father's heart.

We sat and talked about how Sally Clarkson had amazingly, gently mentored us both. How, because of God's grace and Sally's wisdom, we both were growing into mothers who didn't reflect our path but reflected our purpose.

How I was coming to realize:

My kids don't need to see a supermama. They need to see a mama who needs a Super God. That maybe being the mama I wanted to be wasn't so much about *being* more but *believing* more; believing and trusting more in the God of Hagar and Ruth and Hannah, the God who sees me, who nourishes me, who hears me and answers.

That godly parenting isn't ultimately a function of rules but having a relationship with an ultimate God. That godly parenting is fuelled by God's grace, not my efforts.

That maybe it all comes down to this: if I make God first and am most satisfied in His love, I'm released to love my children fully and most satisfactorily.

Sarah Mae met my own mama that day, and we all hugged and laughed and thanked the Lord for how He is writing our stories, raising hope from ashes—for us and our children.

And now, sitting here in the ER with my mama, working at every breath, my mama reaching over and lovingly patting my shoulder, I hold these pages, words of Sarah Mae's and Sally's, that are a gift to every mother, that welcome mothers everywhere out of hiding and loneliness and into a fellowship of sisters and mentors. That will make you feel not alone; that will make you feel there is real God-given hope.

That will make you feel there is space to breathe in your own longing, to beautifully answer this vocation of motherhood.

Biblical scholars note that the name of God, the letters YHWH, sounds like the sound of our breathing—aspirated consonants. God Himself names Himself, and He names Himself that which is the sound of our own breathing.

And this book?

Is exactly what you need if you just need to breathe.

Is exactly what you need if you just need to keep saying His name.

Ann Voskamp, mama to six, author of the
New York Times bestseller *One Thousand Gifts: A Dare to Live Fully Right Where You Are*
ER waiting room, October 2012

Introduction: "I Can't Be a Mother Today"

Anxiety struck me immediately. It was too early to be up, but "too early" didn't matter to my sweet little boy who was ready for the day the minute the sun shone through his bedroom window. My daughter Caroline needed milk and a new diaper, and all three of my little ones were, of course, hungry.

After forcing myself to sit up, I stared at the wall, then fell back down into my bed. I pulled my knees to my chest and the blanket over my head as tears came down and these words tumbled out to my God: "I can't be a mother today, Lord, I'm just too tired."

Getting awakened multiple times a night, every night, is enough to make anyone crash, but add the weight of having to function throughout the day in order to take care of a one-, two-, and four-year-old, and this mama was spent before the day began. Just knowing the strength and energy that would be required to make it through the day was enough to sway me to stay balled up under warm covers. Serious sleep deprivation combined with the constant giving of myself, soothing cries, breaking up fights, training, disciplining, and trying to stay calm and gentle in the middle of it all was breaking me. I needed help. I so badly needed someone to call who could come and rescue me, just for one day. But that wasn't my reality.

My mom was ill and living in Florida, my mother-in-law had a full-time job, and there was no money to hire someone to help me out for a couple hours a month, so I could get a break. My husband took over sometimes, but he was tired too, and we wanted weekends to be with each other. Plus, there was nowhere to go even if I could get out because money was tight; coffee at a coffee shop was a luxury out of my reach. It sounds like a lot of excuses, but the point is that I felt very alone, and very, very tired. Depression snuck up on me; there was a shell of a woman where I once was. My ideals, my hopes, my joy were snatched away before I had a chance to notice. Pleas for help aimed at heaven seemed to be met with silence. The message was clear: this was my life, and I needed to just deal with it.

Adjusting didn't go well. Anger and resentment were living just under my skin. Exhausted, out of my mind, and still hormonal, every day felt like a fight. Feelings of desperation were like an ever-present shadow over the good in my life. Experiencing hope in Jesus felt like chasing gold at the end of a rainbow . . . getting to it was always out of reach. Motherhood was something I planned for, something I wanted, so why was living it out so drastically different from my expectations?

Down to the bone, to the deepest part of my soul, is the love I have for my children. Every day of my life is imperfectly offered to them. But the little years, they're hard and oftentimes lonely. It's like a secret we fear sharing, just how life-altering motherhood is, especially when you don't have training or support. Let me pull back the curtain on the idea that just because you love and are thankful to be a mother, parenting will come easily or naturally. The lifetime commitment that is motherhood will, many days, stretch you beyond what you think you can handle.

We moms don't need an instruction manual. We need physical help.

If you're a mom of little ones and you don't have very much help, I know you're struggling to breathe. Your days morph into your nights and mornings come too quickly. You're bone-tired and would give just about anything for a break, a soul-filling, relaxing, *quiet* break. You need to be pampered. I've been there, and if it weren't for an unexpected gift, I'm not sure you'd be reading these words today. Let me share the gift with you.

Sally Clarkson was just the name on a book.

I knew *of* her because sitting on my bookshelf was one of her books. Her philosophies inspired me, and in her was a source of wisdom that my life longed for. She said yes when I asked her to speak at a conference I hosted. After the conference, Sally pursued me.

She would call me and tell me that the Lord had placed me on her heart. Insecurities led me to believe that she was just being nice and that eventually her calls would stop. But they didn't stop, and we began a friendship, one that still fills me with awe. How did I get a friend and mentor who cares for me this much? It's a grace-gift to be given a wise woman mentor, especially when you least expect it.

After several challenging and life-giving conversations, I decided to leave my home and go to Colorado to spend a week with Sally and her family. I had not been away from my babies for more than two days at a time, so this trip was one of faith, fear, and prayer. I didn't want to leave my family, but I knew Sally was going to give me something I needed to continue on as a mama;

she was going invest in my life as a Titus 2 woman, and she was going to pamper me.

> Older women likewise are to be reverent in their behavior, not malicious gossips nor enslaved to much wine, teaching what is good, so that they may encourage the young women to love their husbands, to love their children, to be sensible, pure, workers at home, kind, being subject to their own husbands, so that the word of God will not be dishonored. (Titus 2:3–5)

Being in Colorado changed me. It was there that I realized how desperate I was to breathe. The first night I was in Sally's home, I slowly got into a great-smelling bed (clean sheets!) that was all prepared for me, and I cozied down and stretched out knowing I would get a full night's sleep. I savored this moment of knowing that I was actually going to rest. As my head lay on the pillow, I inhaled deeply and exhaled with a smile. Rest. Quiet. I didn't know how much I needed Colorado, or Sally, or this perfect-smelling bed. But I did. And it was so, so good. Sally cared for me, nurtured me, took me out for a grand breakfast, and invited me to enter my life with a sense of beauty and thrill. Sally gave me the courage to go home and be a willing participant in my life.

Now here I am writing this book with my mentor and friend. When the first words to this book were typed, I was knee-deep in feelings of desperation. Writing this book has been therapy for me. Sally would read some of my writing and then say, "I think you're really depressed, let's talk about this." And we'd talk and she'd give me Scripture and wisdom. I worked out many of my struggles writing this book, and now I feel like I'm at the other end of a tunnel, breaking free into light. I'm in a new season. Wisdom is my companion, and leaning into God is my hope.

My youngest is three now and is sleeping through the night.

You know what this means, right? My nights have been filled with uninterrupted sleep! It is a glorious thing to experience a full night's sleep. Looking back on those desperate days and looking at where I am now, I can confidently say, *"It gets better!"* If only I could have seen that during the hardest times, hope would have been so much easier to grasp.

Friends, fellow mamas, this book is for you.

Sally and I want to encourage you to keep going even when it feels like you can't, and we want to help you. We won't offer you formulas, but we will offer ideas, perspectives, transparency, and wisdom. We have some ideas for you in getting help, and we are making a plea for older women to remember the tired years and come alongside young mothers, so that our children and our children's children will know how to serve and to receive help.

Thank you for giving us your precious, little time. We pray our offerings will not just comfort you but will refresh your soul and spur you on in hope! Do you have your coffee or tea? This time is for you. Let's begin, together.

For a video on this Introduction, scan this QR code with your smart phone or visit http://bit.ly/RfH0tP.

Section 1

The Dream Life . . . Altered

Dear Sally,

I'm really struggling with being a mom today. I feel overwhelmed and underprepared. What if I fail my kids? I'm so scared of messing up. Can I really do this motherhood thing well? Can I really love my children the way they need me to? I feel so inadequate today. Please tell me I'll eventually settle into motherhood with an assurance that I can be a good mom.

Love, Sarah Mae

Sweet Friend,

Almost all mothers I know started out overwhelmed and eventually found their legs and began to create a rhythm in their lives. Please do not allow the guilt or inadequacies you are feeling to overwhelm your life. Jesus is so very gentle. As I learned to be patient with myself as He was and gave myself time to grow and stretch in my ability to mother well, I found that my heart slowly became more filled with love for my children and I experienced a deep fulfillment I never thought was possible. You see, the process of learning how to nurture our children usually always ends up crafting a bigger and more generous soul within us and becomes a grace and beauty to our souls. If you give yourself time to learn and be kind to yourself, you will surely find answers as well as an elegance and refinement that take place in your own soul as He crafts you more into the image of Jesus in the process.

I am praying for you today!

Fondly, Sally

CHAPTER 1

Ideals and Going Under

Sarah Mae

I had it all figured out; my life, you know. I was excited to be a mom, a hands-on mom, a fun, good mom. I was going to teach and train my babes, spend days enjoying their laughter and curious little minds. We'd bake cookies together, read all day when it rained, play for hours, do crafts, and dance every morning. Oh yes, I knew how it was going to be because I was going to create that picture. The vision was fixed in my mind and my heart, the vision of the woman, wife, and mama I was going to be. The woman who occupied my mind was lipstick and familiar perfume, pancakes and smiles, singing and a gentle voice.

She was up early preparing for the day, all dressed, hair done, cute shoes on. She was kind. And she always had her quiet time as the sun rose, breaking the dark into light . . . she was light. Good, nearly perfect. Oh yes, I would be this woman, the woman that my children needed.

This woman, this idealized '50s cliché of perceived security and togetherness, was what I clung to. This vision of the lipstick pancake mama somehow warmed my heart and made me long for what I never had. My mom was the opposite of my dream. She was cigarettes and oatmeal at the babysitter's, alcohol and cutting words, inappropriate and lost. She was a woman who succumbed to the only way she knew how to make it through this hard life. She chose alcohol to get her through, so that is the smell I remember when I think of her. She wasn't bad; she was wounded. Her own pain came out in sarcastic, unnurturing, unsympathetic, unmotherly ways. Because of all the wounds she instilled in me, I threw out all the good that came with her, all the fun and free-spiritedness. She was everything I was not going to be, I vowed it. I loved her; I just didn't want to be her.

I was determined to be the "good" mom, the straight arrow, responsible and loving, always mature and wise. I would be that woman on the cover of the 1950's *Good Housekeeping* magazine. I thought I had a choice to be her, to be me, wrapped in her. Yes, that's what my children needed, because that's what I needed.

I thought I could wrap myself up in an image, but I couldn't, because that picture wasn't real. When it finally dawned on me that I couldn't be my vision of what a "good mom" was, my little world of "perfect" came undone. It was like someone punched me in the gut when, no matter how much I tried, I couldn't be my ideal. I felt tired all the time. I didn't get up early or even get dressed sometimes until the afternoon. I was a terrible housekeeper. Lipstick? Forget it. I was a woman lost, grasping for air, and with nothing to hold on to, I fell flat. Discouragement, depression, and hopelessness surrounded me.

The days became long and impossible. Taking care of my children was too hard. Being a good wife was too hard. Cleaning, creating life, living . . . was just too hard.

My ideals dropped one by one, as the days turned into blurs of time that I couldn't contain. I went from a super-motivated, driven mama to a "don't-get-me-out-of-bed-I'm-depressed" zombie. Because I couldn't achieve my unrealistic goals, I became lifeless and depressed. I didn't even want to try anymore. "Why bother?" I found myself saying over and over again, "I'll just mess up again." I was in a sad state, and I desperately needed someone to speak truth into my life. That's why this book is so important to me. I want to share the experiences I've gone through and am going through as a young mama because I want you to know that you're not alone, that there is so much hope waiting around the bend. I promise you.

Good Ideals

Many of my ideals were good, but the standard I set for myself to meet them was completely unrealistic. A good mom, in my mind, was up bright and early before her children woke up; she got dressed, did her hair, put on her makeup, had her quiet time, and had breakfast simmering in the pan as she went to wake up her babes. Of course in my fantasy she was always cheery, always smelled good, and never raised her voice. She was what God never asked us to be apart from Him: perfect.

What was I thinking? And why didn't someone set me straight?

The reason it hurt so much when I couldn't live up to my ideal was because I had imposed an impossible standard on myself. I forgot that I am a complex human being who has a sin problem. And so do my babes! I didn't take into account my personality, my weaknesses, or my strengths. Rather, I just chose an image and purposed to be that image. I didn't purpose to be Sarah Mae, a unique individual with gifts and talents from God. I didn't even purpose to be who God wanted me to be. Without a realistic vision, I was crushed before the season of motherhood even began.

It was immaturity and an idealistic spirit that led me to think I had motherhood figured out. I like my idealistic spirit, and I want to hold on to it because it's part of how God weaved me together, but I don't want to get snared into the assumption that all my ideals will be just as I envisioned them. Rather, I want to see my ideals as guideposts to look to. I want to set realistic goals that fit who I am, and what God requires of me. I want to always say, "Lord, what do you say?"

And above all, I need to remember that "good" motherliness has nothing to do with how God sees me. Nothing. I am pleasing to Him on my good days and my bad days. His love for me never wavers . . . and never will. Because I'm His.

Sally

Enthroned in an overstuffed chair, I was surrounded by a sea of pink—tissue paper, ribbons and bows, baby booties, tiny lace dresses, and rose-budded sleepers. My heart was swirling with idealistic and peaceful dreams of my coming daughter and me. Beloved friends of all ages had come together to throw a shower for my highly anticipated baby girl, soon to be born.

"Oh, you'll be the perfect mother!"

"Don't worry about her birth, it will all be over so quickly, and after all, you seem so prepared!"

They were certainly right about that. I had carefully read all the baby books, attended all the birthing classes, and eaten all the right foods in all the right months of development. I had practiced repeatedly the correct way to breathe during labor, packed my overnight luggage and diaper bag with all the extra needed baby items, and decorated my baby's room with great skill. I was fairly confident I had everything under control.

After I collected all of my newfound treasures and said my thank-you's, I started down the hall to make my exit. As I slipped out of the room, a woman I barely recognized as a member of my church was very intentionally waiting in the hallway to corner me.

"Sally, I feel I owe it to you to warn you about what is ahead. All of those easy-schmeasy comments about giving birth and having a baby and being a mother are just lies. You are going to hurt like you never imagined during labor and your first weeks are going to be harder than you ever thought. I just wanted to warn you that this is the hardest thing you have probably ever done in your life, and if you are not ready for it to be hard, you will become quite depressed!"

What a thing to say to me at my baby shower! I just brushed off her comments as extreme and assumed she was a serial whiner. As I made my way outside, I whispered a prayer for her under my breath, "Please, Lord, bless this poor woman and help her to grow a healthier attitude!"

Fast-forward to my daughter Sarah's birth: twenty-two straight hours of labor, and more pain than I thought possible. Sarah was stuck in the birth canal for two and a half hours, and so eventually a doctor had to perform an emergency removal using forceps. There was a seemingly endless amount of grunting, groaning, twisting, and drugs just to get her out.

Yet the moment she was placed into my hands, I was filled with such awe and surprise at this baby—*my own* sweet, precious baby—who was in *my* arms. Her little face was battered, but her dark blue eyes were looking pensively toward my voice. I was smitten—and a little shocked as well. I don't know what I was expecting, but it seemed so much more of a miracle to me than I ever had imagined. I fell in love instantly.

"I'm so sorry, but we must take your baby away from you for a little while. She failed the AGPAR test and could be having some severe problems."

After three hours of immense anxiety, my normally straight-faced, bearded doctor walked into the room and said with an exhausted sigh, "I am so sorry, but Sarah's lungs are filled with meconium and she is not breathing very well. She seems to have some other mysterious issues, and I am afraid you will not be able to hold her or have her with you for at least a couple of days."

After all of the anticipation, excitement, and planning, my hopes and dreams were dashed and my mother-heart was already broken. As my husband, Clay, wheeled me through the hallway passing happy, smiling moms showing their sweet babies off to admiring relatives and friends, I felt the intense pain of heartbreak, of having nothing but the sadness of empty hands.

The next time I saw Sarah, it was only through a thick, protective glass wall, and I could see her pathetic little body surging up and down as she gasped for breath. Oxygen tubes were in her nose, monitors were strapped to her fragile, tiny body, and tubes were seemingly everywhere.

This was hardly the entrance into motherhood of which I had long dreamed.

To make it worse, I developed the flu while I was in the hospital and became quickly dehydrated. Consequently, my milk never came in.

"Some women just don't have the right kind of breasts," the self-important nurse commented to me as we watched baby Sarah strain at her first bottle of formula, amidst tubes and constraints. Just the words I needed to make me feel even more insecure! In retrospect, I wish I had reported the surly nurse to the hospital—just what are the right kinds of breasts?

Finally, three days after her birth, after what seemed like an eternity of complications and challenges, I was able to take my sweet first child back to our home. As I sat in the faint light of an early morning in our little den, I held my precious little one ever so tenderly, feeling very isolated and alone. Little did I know that this moment would signify a pivotal moment in my life as a mother.

Fear flooded my heart, and the insecure thoughts began to surge in. *What if I don't know how to take care of her? What if she gets pneumonia?* Anxiety wrapped around my whole being and sent me into a hole of insecurity. I had no parents to advise me until later that week, and in their own raising of my siblings and me, they had taken all the detached routes—no nursing, attaching, or nurturing. There was no one to give me the kind of advice I was longing to hear or validation for my newfound ideals from all the books I had read.

As I sat in the still darkness, my heart cried out to God, perhaps more sincerely than ever before.

"Lord, teach me how to be a mother. I feel so inadequate. I don't know what to do. But you are Sarah's heavenly Father, and you love her even more than I do, so please show me your way and help me to know how to do the right things."

This is the true beginning point—God. He is the one who created babies bursting with life and the mamas who love to care and watch over them. He brought forth from His imagination the most beautiful of gardens, threw galaxies of stars into orbit, and painted our world with color. In keeping with His character, He must have intended something beautiful in creating a woman with this ability to give life, nurture with love, and cultivate the soul of a precious human being entrusted into her hands.

Each of us has a story, but God, who originated the design of motherhood, is the expert advisor to whom we should turn. God has equipped us for every good work, and I am quite confident that He who designed this role to be so eternally significant is the one who is ready to help, support, instruct, and guide. He will provide all we need for the task He has given us to fulfill. But to hear from God we must become women of the Word and women who pray, so that His voice may lead us as we grow into this role with grace. I look back now through all of the huge obstacles, unexpected twists, and challenges on this course of motherhood through my life and see that at each point, He was there, helping, carrying, guarding, and blessing as a true and present advocate. He is the reason for any success or blessing I have felt as a mother.

As I sat in my little den, unsure of either my or my daughter's future, I gave little Sarah into God's hands, put her at my breast to attempt nursing, and by faith rested in this new assurance that this place called motherhood would become a new pathway in my life. I caught a glimpse of God's longing to teach me more about His ways and His grace as I accepted this gift He had given into my keeping, my very own little girl. It was here that great thoughts and inspiration began to be birthed, as I held my precious one and pondered in the presence of the Lord what He had in mind for mothers.

In this culture of quick satisfaction and gratification, many of us have never been taught to believe that someday we will have to give an account to God, face-to-face, for the spiritual, emotional, and moral work that we steward in the lives of our children. The souls of our children will last for all eternity, and if we believe Scripture to be true, the way we shepherd them will undoubtedly have repercussions far beyond our lives here on earth. As I searched Scripture in my own walk as a young mom, I began to catch a glimpse of the profound meaning imbued by God into the home environment. My identity as a mother would be wrapped up inextricably in the very place in which my moral character would be formed. My home, then, became my kingdom over which I longed to rule well as I was crafting lives, my own children, for His glory.

This kingdom of home is the place of refuge, comfort, and inspiration. It is a rich world where great souls can be formed, and from which men and women of great conviction and dedication can emerge. It is the place where the models of marriage, love, and relationship are emulated and passed on to the next generation. One of the great losses of this century is the lost imagination for what the home can be if shaped by the creative hand of God's Spirit.

When I considered the role of motherhood as well as the shaping of my children into warriors for His kingdom purposes, I walked by necessity through the questions of what it means to take on the calling of motherhood and to embrace home as a place of such great potential. Becoming a mother is a role that most women are ill-prepared for or ill-trained to understand, yet it has such vast consequences in the course and direction of history. I have even come to believe that a mother's role might be the most determining factor as to how history will unfold.

Understanding that the best and most lasting "work" I would ever do was wrapped up in my call as a mother gave me a grand scope for my life such as I had never known before. I began to see that the nurturing of my children was my great stewardship in every part of their little lives: accepting them into my arms and bearing the responsibility of their very health from feeding at my breasts; developing their emotional well-being by encouraging them to attach deeply to me as infants; stimulating their brains by talking with them, touching them, snuggling with them; and predisposing them to know the love of God by building pathways in their brains. I was just beginning to grasp how profound God had created the role of a mother to be.

However, when I look back now on the grand scheme of things, I can see clearly that motherhood is a process, a journey. It was fraught with so many moments and days of failure, anger, stress, and exhaustion. Little by little, I have learned grace, joy, patience, and hope, and slowly my soul is being shaped into His image. I wouldn't trade the journey or my ideals for any other life. But I couldn't have known any of this starting out. I hope in the following chapters that I might help you see the bigger picture, that as you pursue this beautiful design that God planned from the beginning, you will find deep fulfillment and lasting affirmation that will serve you the rest of your life.

Your Turn

Isaiah 41:10: "Do not fear, for I am with you; do not anxiously look about you, for I am your God. I will strengthen you, surely I will help you, surely I will uphold you with My righteous right hand."

- Remember, a woman who is alone in motherhood becomes a target of discouragement for Satan. Are you alone in your role as a mother?

- If God created you to be a mother and is present with you each step of the way, how should that make a difference in your role as a mom?

Matthew 11:28: "Come to Me, all who are weary and heavy-laden, and I will give you rest."

- Does God understand and know when you are weary?

- How do you find rest amidst this exhausting journey of motherhood?

- Where is your source of strength?

Something to Do

Take time to get away with your Bible and a journal. After pondering these verses, make a list of all that is causing you fear, anxiety, or weariness. Then write a prayer to God, and give up all of your burdens of motherhood into His hands. Ask God to give you strength, rest, and wisdom in the specific areas you need it. Date your prayer and determine to look for His help and guidance every day in this journey of motherhood, because He is with you.

For a video on chapter 1, scan this QR code with your smart phone or visit http://bit.ly/SgNcSi.

Dear Sally,

I've taken personality tests that say I'm an off-the-chart extrovert, but I don't feel so extroverted anymore. I just want to be alone more and more these days. I'm so tired, and in the evening I just want to rest. I know I need friends and community, but when? How? I'm tired.

Love, SM

Dearest Sarah,

We were crafted by God to have friends. Motherhood was meant to be experienced with other mothers, aunts, grandmothers, and a community of women sharing the load. Please do not attempt this alone! Find an older woman and ask her to mentor you. Create a play group with other young moms and build your fellowship and fun over the same ideals—maybe study a book together or have a mom's night out. And remember, a wise woman is one who copies wise women. I surround myself with wise friends and make time to encourage my heart with such friends, so I can have wisdom for this task. A friend is made to help you shoulder this incredible job. And remember, I will be here for you!

Love, Sally

CHAPTER 2
The Go-It-Alone Culture (On Needing People)

Sarah Mae

I have read tons of parenting books. Because I've read so many parenting books, I thought that I could take the information, absorb it, implement it seamlessly, and be an expert on parenting—this all before I had children. I really was convinced that I could gain enough knowledge to get me through motherhood. I believed that if I just did what I was told via parenting expert authors, I would excel at being a mother.

Ha!

After I had my first daughter, I was convinced I was an ace mother. All except for the incessant crying every evening between 7 p.m. and 11 p.m., I was on top of my game. I made time for my husband, I kept a fairly clean house, and I played with my sweet little girl throughout the day. I also had her listen to classical music, of course. After five months of nighttime crying, I finally got her into a routine (thank you, Jesus), and life became optimal. She was in bed at six thirty every evening, and she took three naps a day. I thought all babies did that. Life went along swimmingly, except for some boredom during the days, and I had plenty of free time, which I spent reading more parenting books and developing a hefty pridefulness in my excellent mothering abilities.

When my little girl was ten months old, I found out I was pregnant with baby number two. We were so happy to welcome a boy into our family just nineteen months after Ella was born. My mother-in-law came and stayed with me for a whole week to take care of me and watch Ella while I assimilated myself with Caed. He was an easy baby, and such a good sleeper, which was a good thing because I couldn't pay quite as much attention to him since I had Ella to care for as well.

I was so tired with those two babes. In fact, I started drinking coffee after I had my son. Coffee was a great pick-me-up and it got me through the long mornings that began when I woke up, the babes at six thirty every morning; I got them up, so I could put them to bed early. Oh yes, I was an expert on scheduling then, which is ironic since I am not a scheduled person myself. I am carefree and moment by moment, but I was determined to do right by my children, despite my own bad habits. I pushed through and maintained, but then I was not only tired, I was lonely. My husband had friends and things to do, but I felt like I had nothing. None of my friends had children. I went to the library and participated in some moms and kids groups, but I needed something for myself.

My husband played softball, and I began to resent him for it. I did the independent makeup consultant thing for a while, but eventually realized it wasn't good for me, so I quit. I took out my frustrations and feelings of loneliness on my husband. Every time he left me to go to a softball game or see a friend, I got angry. One day he finally said to me, "You need a hobby." He was willing to give me time away from the kids, but I felt lost. I didn't know what I wanted or what to do with myself. So I kept on pouring into the babes, preparing homeschool ideas and materials (even though they were only one and two years old!). That's when I found out about blogs, online websites written by moms like me who offered encouragement. I learned all I could from these mamas, and eventually I decided I wanted to do what they did—I wanted to blog. Blogging would be my hobby. I found great joy writing on my blog in the evenings after my babes were in bed; writing gave me an outlet, and it felt refreshing to be an encouragement to other mamas in the same life boat as myself. My children were going to bed early, I was writing, and I finally felt like I was in control.

Then along came Caroline, my beautiful, feisty Caroline. She blew all of my "expertness" out of the water. At first, she was this delicate little doll of a baby, sweet and mostly easy. Then she turned two.

All of a sudden, my sweet little Caroline turned into a wild fire. All of my "I'm such a good mom, I did everything right, you should do what I do" mentality was totally shattered. My son had tested my resolve quite a few times with his stubbornness, but Caroline? She was in a league of her own, and life felt out of control. One minute I was Mrs. Expert-in-Control mom, and the next I was falling fast, feeling waves of pressure and mounting responsibility. My children were staying up later, they were exerting their wills, and my control began to slip. Failure loomed over me as I realized I couldn't seem to catch up with my ideals. I made lists, read books, and tried harder, but I just kept failing at doing all the things I wanted to do: keep up on the kiddos' chores, teach scripture, play games, read books, train and discipline, clean the dishes, keep up with the laundry, keep my husband happy, etc. All of these noble goals became too much, and I gave in to being tired and depressed. Feeling like a failure as a wife and a mama, I just sort of gave up; I stopped being motivated to try. I was totally overwhelmed; I was drowning.

What happened to my resolve, my strong ideals and convictions? I still loved my children completely and wanted the best for them, but something was dying inside me. I didn't feel like the vibrant woman I used to be; I felt dull.

I wish someone would have told me, tried to prepare me, for just how hard motherhood would be.

When things got really bad, I tried to reach out for help in small ways, but I never wanted to put anyone else out, so I would act like I was fine. In reality, I was getting worse. I wasn't spending time with friends, I didn't have anyone to watch the babes, so I could get out or go on a date with my husband, and I was lost in a wreckage of undisciplined activity. I thought I could do this mothering thing without other women, but it turned out, I couldn't. I needed help; I needed a mentor.

Sally is God's grace to me. God providentially brought her into my life when my children were two, three, and five years old, and she was persistent in getting my attention. When I finally accepted that she sincerely wanted to encourage and help me, I could feel blessings pouring down on me. She became my mentor, but she also became my friend and my advocate.

We need advocates. An advocate is someone who goes to bat for you, who watches out for you and protects you. That person is on your side and wants the best for you.

If you don't have a mentor or a friend or advocate in your life right now who teaches and encourages your spirit, I want you to stop reading and start praying right now. Ask God specifically for what you need as a mama of little ones. I don't know when He'll answer that prayer, or how, but I know He will answer. Be patient. I prayed for years, but when my prayer was answered, it was better than I could have imagined it.

Sally

"Two are better than one because they have a good return for their labor. For if either of them falls, the one will lift up his companion. But woe to the one who falls when there is not another to lift him up."

ECCLESIASTES 4:9–10

Going at it alone is, without a doubt, one of the most common and effective strategies that Satan uses to discourage moms. A woman alone in her home with her ideals eventually wears down and becomes a perfect target for Satan to discourage. Some women have journeyed alone for so long they are not even aware of their urgent need for mentors, friends, peers, and fellowship.

My own story involves many such moments. Early in my walk as a mother, I often felt quite despondent and in need of the gift of friendship. Moving seventeen times, six times internationally, created for me a legacy of many years of loneliness, feelings of being invisible, and a lack of support systems or encouragement from other young moms. We are living in an isolationist culture today and have become accustomed to lonely living that God never intended us to experience. I often felt the keen sting of modern culture's unfamiliar and hostile isolation.

God made us for community and accountability and close friendship. He also created family, so that no one would ever have to be alone or bear the burden of life by themselves. Families were designed by God to include moms and dads, grandparents, cousins, aunts and uncles, and a whole host of people who would walk alongside you, committed to you through the passages of life. Young moms were never meant to be without the advice and care of multiple women assisting them and advising them in their lives.

Yet we have become so used to living without support that we often lose perspective on how much we need intimate friendships with other women. This deep need sometimes puts pressure on husbands to fulfill needs that they were never designed to fill. No matter how wonderful a man may be, he is not crafted by God to meet all of a woman's needs. Through the centuries, women in the home usually had a mom, aunt, sister, or grandmother living close by. They would walk out their back door and talk to each other as they hung clothing on the clothes line or shared a cup of tea while their children played together outdoors. Families living in community generally had the same values and faith and could pass on a legacy of confidence and security to the children and young moms.

Once, I was visiting a new town where we were thinking of moving. A friend of mine had asked one of her friends if I could stay with her while I was looking for a home for our family. I had three of my young children with me, having left Clay and my oldest back home. On the first morning of our arrival, I awoke before my children, which was rare, and slipped down the stairs to the kitchen to have a cup of tea. As I walked into the kitchen, there was a tray with a candle lit, a pot of tea, two pumpkin muffins, a tiny little vase with a pink rosebud in it, and a card that said, "Sally, I have prayed for you today, that you would know God's love, His provision, and His blessing as you move to a new home. We are looking so forward to having you as our friend in Colorado." Below this note were written the words, "May the peace of the Lord be with you, for He is near."

Unexpectedly, the tears began flowing down my face. I was so used to toughing it out and taking care of all of our family's needs and losing sleep and caring for the kids alone that I didn't even know how much I needed a real live friend who could communicate to me that I was not invisible, and show me thoughtfulness that comes from a heart moved by the Spirit of God. Even just the thought that someone else had been considerate of me and prepared my breakfast touched a very deep and vulnerable place in my heart that I had not even recognized as a need. The three days I stayed with this wonderful, life-giving woman filled my emotional cup and gave me a new outlook on life. We eventually became the best of friends, simply because she took the time to initiate toward me, perceive my needs, and serve me.

None of us are made to deal with life alone. All of us, even introverts, are made for relationship, to experience God's grace through our dearest friends around us. Realizing how important this need was, I made a long list of groups that I would start or join wherever I moved. The first step when I was in a new town would be to find a group of moms and attend activities at a church. As I would get to know some women and families, I would initiate a coffee time together to get to know these moms. Then I would extend an invitation to my home for a "mom's night out." It would usually involve something as simple as lighting a candle, putting out something hot to drink and a small snack on the table, and inviting a friend to join me in fellowship in an environment in which the Lord could show up.

Sometimes these groups grew and became large, and sometimes my meetings would fizzle and I would need to search elsewhere to find a kindred spirit. But I learned that I had to become an initiator if I wanted to have friends and fellowship for myself, as well as for Clay and the kids. Having a friend who shared my ideals was essential to my own well-being and the emotional health of my family.

At times, I started a small support system with a couple of other families. Even now, as my children have grown up and moved out, we have two families that we have consistently met with for dinner once a month for about five years. Over time they have become some of my dearest friends. We started out as a play group with our children, meeting at the park or going on fun outings together. Eventually these families started serving at our ministry conferences and all of us began to knit our hearts together in ministry, life, and holidays.

Now our children consider them as part of our family, and we gather on holidays to share progressive meals, where we go for a different course at each home. Our children have built a legacy of memories through serving, traveling, celebrating, and enjoying life together as they have grown up. We have had ups and downs in our relationships, but our hearts and souls have bonded through the sharing of life.

I have had to start almost every group to which I have ever belonged. One of the first lessons I learned was to not be discouraged if others did not invite me. In this individualistic culture where everyone is too busy and overwhelmed with life, the groups in which we find community will inevitably be the groups we start ourselves.

Cultivating friendships is a real talent and skill developed by mature and wise women of God. With practice, it becomes an art of love. By involving myself and my children in the lives of others, my children have benefitted so very much in their own development. They needed more than just Clay and me to speak into their lives, to love them, pray with them, and have fun with them. By building these groups of connectivity over the years, we learned to provide a "positive peer pressure." My children were no longer required to bear Clay's and my ideals and biblical standards alone anymore, but instead they were provided with a host of friends and families who believe what we believe. That has been a strength to every single member of my family; it causes the strands of our life-accountability to be stronger and more effective.

Over the years I have established a strategy of developing different groups.

First, I always look for a few women my age or who have children the ages of my children. This will give you friends who will know about events in your area that are suited to your stage in life, give your children friends to play with at the park, and connect you with people who might want to trade kids for that much-needed date night or time out alone.

Next, I look for an older woman in church or in a ministry whom I think might stimulate me spiritually. I was in a small group Bible study the first year I moved to Colorado and fell in love with one of the older women. I asked her to breakfast at my home and we began to develop a friendship. Now I try to meet with her at least once a month when we are both in town. I know that when I am with her, I will be more encouraged to love God, to be a better mom, and to be a better spouse, because I know that this woman walks with God.

Finally, I find a mom or woman who is younger than I to befriend, who is looking for encouragement. I vowed to the Lord that I would seek out younger women in whom to invest my life and time because I had so longed for such fellowship and friendship when I was starting out. I have found that when I feel responsible to encourage other younger moms in their walk with God and in biblical ideals, I am more encouraged myself to live up to the standards that I am teaching.

As I look at my present life, I am amazed at what a plethora of friends I now have, when for so many years I felt isolated, bored, and empty. It has certainly taken a good deal of work and many years of investment, but, as a result, I have my cup filled with the joy of strong fellowship. This year when Clay had surgery, I was surprised to find that every night for three weeks we had a hot meal waiting at our door. I didn't ask for anyone to cook for us, but from years of investing in lives, God has given me a support system that I never had with my own family.

Your Turn

Ecclesiastes 4:9–12: "Two are better than one because they have a good return for their labor. For if either of them falls, the one will lift up his companion. But woe to the one who falls when there is not another to lift him up. Furthermore, if two lie down together they keep warm, but how can one be warm alone? And if one can overpower him who is alone, two can resist him. A cord of three strands is not quickly torn apart."

- Friendship has always been a strength of women, and yet we live in a very isolationist culture. What are the consequences when a woman does not have a companion to help her?

- What is an answer to keeping from falling down in the trials of life and motherhood, and how can you develop a network of friends to walk beside you in this journey so you will not be alone?

Titus 2:3–5: "Older women likewise are to be reverent in their behavior, not malicious gossips nor enslaved to much wine, teaching what is good, so that they may encourage the young women to love their husbands, to love their children, to be sensible, pure, workers at home, kind, being subject to their own husbands, so that the word of God will not be dishonored."

- Mentoring from someone more experienced and wiser is always a great help in almost any field of education or ideals. Who is most likely to be able to help you have perspective in your journey as a mom, according to this verse?

- What are the specific areas you are supposed to make your focus as a woman of God?

Something to Do

List some women in your sphere of influence who are at the same basic stage of life and motherhood. Gather these friends at your home or a coffee shop, and tell them about your need to have friends who will walk beside you. Ask them if they would be willing to meet once a month to encourage one another or to read and discuss a book on motherhood and to provide fellowship for one another.

Having friends who encourage me to be the best I can be is a legacy I give myself. Think of one or two older women whom you have met at church or whom you admire. Ask them out to coffee and share with them your need for a friend who is ahead of you on this journey of motherhood. Ask them specifically for help or accountability, and ask if they would meet with you during a specific time once or twice a month to talk, pray, and give you accountability.

For a video on chapter 2, scan this QR code with your smart phone or visit http://bit.ly/TEGNxh.

Dear Sally,

I really wish there was a formula that had all the right answers on how to raise my kids well. Just yesterday I was so frustrated by my daughter's disobedience. I knew I needed to discipline her, but I wasn't sure how. I've tried different things, but she's so unpredictable. I'm not sure how to function without formulas. I need real, tangible answers. Help?

Love, SM

Hi Sarah,

Just a note today to remind you not to listen to all of those formulas and rules out there. God did not create us to fit into a box. You and your sweet ones, with all of your individual quirks and bents, will express your own unique family culture. Live well within the limitations of your personality and theirs and you will find more joy. Love well and deeply, give yourself and your children lots of grace and forgiveness, and lean deeply into the grace of Christ as you walk this journey. Rules, laws, and boxes tend to kill the soul when it comes to expectations of motherhood. Freedom leads you to more contentment and joy. And in living by faith in this freedom, your heart will be pleasing to God, who is your audience, after all.

Love, Sally

CHAPTER 3

Formulas Don't Always Work

Sarah Mae

She slid, methodically and stealth-like, out of her crib. Once on the outside of her crib bars, she stopped for a moment, leaned her head to the right, and listened. After about ten seconds, she fell purposely to the floor and headed toward her fan in an effort to turn it off. I'm faster, and she didn't see me coming. She jumped and ran back to her crib, but it was too late; I caught her red-handed. I was going to win this battle; she would stay in bed.

Oh, my little Caroline, my feisty, beautiful, wild, smart (did I already say feisty?) Caroline. The two-year-old wonder that made me a humble parent. That girl, we were in a bedtime showdown, as we had been many a night, and she was clearly packing more heat than I was! But I was determined to win. I was going to require obedience, and if she didn't comply, swift discipline would ensue.

After approximately one thousand and one times of Caroline getting out of bed, I was ready to head to the mad house. I would have happily packed my bags and gone to bounce off the white walls. It was that bad. Spanking didn't work, sternness didn't work, ignoring her didn't work, begging and tears didn't work; she laughed in the face of my formula-wielding ways. The only reason she finally fell asleep was because tiredness overcame her. She won. I was defeated. I cried again and again.

The reality sunk in: Caroline was not going to fit in any box. There would be no pat answer for how to raise and discipline her.

I was not prepared to raise an out-of-the-box (as Sally calls her) child.

I love the idea of formulas: the idea that somebody can give me an answer that I can implement to whatever life issue I'm facing and then life will go along just how I want it to. With Caroline, I was told that if I would just do X, Y, and Z, she would obey. If she wasn't obeying, it was my fault; I was doing it wrong. Of course I felt like a terrible mother.

Formulas and Guilt

Formulas don't create guilt, but failing to get the desired result from following formulas most certainly can lead to horrible feelings of inadequacy and guilt: "I must not be doing it enough." "I must not be doing it right." "What am I doing wrong?"

My son is five now, but I could cry just thinking about all the physical discipline we put him through when he was only two and a half. Just remembering and writing these words now bring tears to my eyes and a pain in my heart. He was just a little boy, figuring out his world, and yet we labeled him "stubborn" and were determined to spank him out of it. We weren't cruel; we were lost, and we turned to advice that told us to spank until he obeyed. So we tried it, and my son got angry. He was an angry little boy who believed he was bad. There is darkness in each of us that bends toward rebellion, but his feelings of "bad" had more to do with shame. For him, all the spankings meant that he was no good; he didn't experience the redemption that good discipline brings. He didn't like himself, and he didn't think he could change. All this in the mind and heart of a two-year-old!

I believe those feelings of shame are too heavy a burden for anyone, but especially a child. My son couldn't make sense of them, or see any hope, so he just crumbled in feelings of failure. I knew the spankings couldn't go on; not only was he angry, he had a skewed understanding of the discipline we were giving. It was not heart corrective; it was heart damaging. He may have obeyed, but his spirit was hurting. I wasn't okay with that. My husband and I decided to back off of spanking and instead spend more time with him, listening to him, talking through his areas of sin, and using other methods of discipline. Today, at five years old, my boy is not angry. He is beginning to understand his sinful bents, but he is also becoming aware of the fact that he was created in the image of God and is so loved by Him! He knows we mess up, and we are going to keep messing up, but that there is love in confessing and giving our sin to God.

The only formula I want my children to tuck deep into their hearts is this: God has weaved each of us uniquely, and we are wonderfully made in His image. We have sin-tattered hearts, but Jesus mends them when we lean into Him and trust Him with our lives. There's the formula. Give Him the bad, and He'll give you the beautiful. It's the human story offered by a compassionate God. "Just as a father has compassion on his children, so the Lord has compassion on those who fear Him" (Psalm 103:13).

For the Mama with an Out-of-the-Box or "Stubborn" Child

I can't and will not give you a formula for dealing with your little ones, the ones who sometimes make you feel crazy or leave you crying on the hallway floor. But I can offer suggestions, some things that greatly helped me as I've learned how to slow down and figure out my children.

Love them. Hug them, kiss them, cuddle with them, spend more time rubbing their heads and holding their hands. Give yourself to them without rush. Pray with them, and let them twirl your hair in their little fingers. Look them in the eye when you talk to them.

Give words of affirmation. Tell them, whether you feel it or not, that you delight in them, that they are a delight (if they don't feel like a delight, ask God to give you those feelings). Tell them, "You are beautiful and smart and God loves you. I'm so glad you're my child." Tell them that they can never lose your love, no matter what. And mean it.

Consider several different discipline techniques. Each child responds differently to methods of discipline, and it's important that you study your child and figure out what works with him or her. Our goal is always the heart. We think about how we can help our children understand their sin and then turn and follow good. We want to teach them to love and follow Jesus with their hearts, minds, and souls. These are the important things. Behavior follows the heart.

Remember that you have a bent toward sin just as your little ones do. We all sin, and we all struggle with rebellion. But God loves us, and when we are His, He is pleased with us because of Christ, not because of how little we mess up. He is gracious, compassionate, and faithful. We can approach the throne of grace with confidence; can your children approach you with confidence, knowing they will be loved no matter what? Let them know that you are on their team; that you are for them and not against them; that you will forgive, always, just as the Father forgives.

Lay Your Children at the Foot of the Cross

I love that we mamas tend to follow formulas because it means we are trying to be intentional with our children. We care enough to discipline and teach them! We love them and want to prepare them for the world; we want to teach them how to live well. That is so, so good. But we've got to know that, ultimately, the most important thing is laying our children at the foot of the cross and praying that Jesus will call them to Him. He is the author of their souls, and He is the only one who can reign in a broken soul. So pray for your children and show them Jesus.

Lead them to the One who can intertwine His Spirit with theirs, the One who changes us from the inside out.

> To those . . . who are chosen according to the foreknowledge of God the Father, by the sanctifying work of the Spirit, to obey Jesus Christ and be sprinkled with His blood: May grace and peace be yours in the fullest measure. (1 Peter 1:1–2)

Sally

> *"It was for freedom that Christ set us free; therefore keep standing firm and do not be subject again to a yoke of slavery."*
>
> Galatians 5:1

Sequestered on my floral love seat, looking out on three acres of trees and flowers, I reflected on my life of fifty years. The sun was setting, and out my cozy windowed sun porch I could see peace flooding the valley.

My birthday had been soul-filling. Quiet, but lovely. Clay had arranged a special candlelight dinner at home with just us and our four sweet children. The three older kids, twenty, seventeen, and fifteen, had shared all of the things they appreciated about me—the devotions I had led in the quiet mornings when we would cuddle on the couch; the traveling adventures we took in missions and ministry trips all over the world; the books we all loved and read together; the afternoon teas, backrubs, pizza and movie nights, birthday cinnamon rolls; and the family culture that made us all feel we belonged. Joy, at seven, simply drew me a picture of "Joy and Mama" holding hands, with me labeled as "her best friend."

As I sat there, I was overwhelmed with gratefulness for how God had blessed me during these first fifty years! Our family was intact and loved the Lord, and loved and celebrated life together in close relationship. Clay and I had realized our dream of establishing a ministry together to train families how to reach their children's hearts and to build them into godly leaders. Both of us had been able to have books published with various publishers, as well as start a small publishing house ourselves. We had inaugurated mom conferences all over the world, also a dream come true. And most importantly, God had blessed us with four wonderful children.

But as I was pondering these thoughts, I realized that much of my fulfillment came from moving to "the beat of a different drum." Much of my life had been invested in following God's ideals, which took me directly away from cultural expectations. God took us on grand adventures set out upon by faith, far exceeding what I could have ever expected from my life.

Every family's puzzle will be different. We can only please God if we listen to His call on our lives. Each of us has a different personality, different strengths and limitations, and different passions and stewardships. God gives us great freedom to exercise wisdom and authority in order to rule over our lives and make them productive for our own families.

How grateful I am that at an early age in our Christian lives, my family learned to walk by faith together. Hebrews 11:6 tells us that, "Without faith it is impossible to please Him, for he who comes to God must believe that He is and that He is a rewarder of those who seek Him."

There are all sorts of nonconformists in Scripture: David, a shepherd boy, rising out of his meager social status to kill Goliath, the bane of the Israelite armies; the two spies, Caleb and Joshua, believing that God could deal with the giants and give them the land of milk and honey against the advice of ten other leaders; Moses defeating the Egyptian army by merely stepping into the Red Sea with millions of people following him; Joseph believing in a dream that he would rule over his brothers, and seeing it eventually come to pass through faith in God's promises; Joshua defeating an army merely by marching in a circle around their city. There are, of course, countless other stories of such great faith. None were called to do the logical or expected thing but rather to look to God, listen to His voice, and follow Him.

Often, well-meaning believers felt free to tell us "God's will for our lives," according to them. I call these Job's friends. His "friends" felt their own wills were sovereign over God's individual calling upon Job's life. Though Job was experiencing persecution because he was righteous, and Satan made every effort to squash his faith, God had sovereignly allowed the test, trusting that Job would love Him and remain faithful through it all. Our "Job's friends" would question the dreams that we had, in faith, followed. Early on I realized that all of the times I had found joy and freedom and pleasure in my life were when I listened to God's voice in Scripture and pursued the dreams God had put on my heart. What other people thought of our path was irrelevant.

There was a wide assortment of people whom we disappointed because we didn't fit into their boxes. We didn't meet the expectation of our family, who wished that I had sent my children to a normal school. There were also many "advisors" who felt my idealistic ways in education and discipleship might have severe consequences. We were often asked if it "wasn't possible that we might lead many astray" in our writings, as people might not follow the traditional routes of authoritarian discipline and curricular standard education. Many times we heard the words, "You aren't spanking your children enough!" And yet my darling little Nathan, whom I was later to learn was ADHD and OCD, always responded to me when I was gentle, loving, and filling his cup. He needed patience, and he needed me to like him and believe in him. As an adult, he is a strong man with a great artist's soul, having an impact on his world. I so enjoy him because he is out-of-the-box.

Many of our friends from our time in overseas missions told me authoritatively that two children were enough, and one said that it would be "a waste of my time and training to focus so much on motherhood instead of missions." Others asked why we would leave the mission field and start a ministry to train and instruct families. Weren't we sending the message that families were more important than being involved in missions?

There were so many critics and voices that tempted me to feel insecure about our faith decisions. Whether it was curriculum or discipline, what movies we were watching or music we were listening to, or the clothes we wore, so many rules and formulas were thrust upon us.

I believe that there is no "one right way." God calls each of us to seek Him, to look for His wisdom and to follow where He calls us by faith, and it will be a different story for each family, marriage, and individual mom or dad. To walk that uncertain line, we must trust that God will be faithful to lead and guide us.

Clay and I found that the more we walked with God, the more we felt called to live our own puzzle according to the integrity of the husband, wife, and parents God had made us, within the limitations of our own personalities.

I see so many young women today who live by fear—fear of what others will think, fear of how they might ruin their children, fear of the expectations of other people, fear that they will not fill in all the holes in their children's lives. I also see women who are afraid to be themselves.

Often in this peer-pressured world, a close second-place motivator to fear is legalism, living by rules and works. So many women are exhausting themselves trying to appease everyone's expectations of them. Following every blog and every piece of advice from books, whether good or bad, they are wearing out themselves and their children. It is vitally important for women to learn how to think biblically for themselves instead of being enslaved to other people's thoughts and opinions. To truly follow God with everything in our lives, we must learn to develop discernment.

God is not a cosmic spoil-sport, seeking to wring out every bit of joy and freedom in life. He has created home as a place that is to be enjoyed and celebrated. A home is an environment designed by God's own hand, more than sufficient to prepare children for their adult lives. A mom is exactly the person that her children need; God created it to be that way! A happy mom who is secure in herself and at ease in her life is a rare gift that children love and appreciate. God promises that when we trust in Him and do not give in to fear and pressure, He will be with us. "The fear of man brings a snare, but he who trusts in the Lord will be exalted" (Proverbs 29:25).

Plan What Kind of Family You Want to Be

Determine for yourself what you hope to be the outcome of your family. What legacies do you want to leave for your children? Clay and I knew we wanted to pass on to our children the strengths we had nurtured in our own lives. We wanted them to know how to think clearly, and so we chose a pathway that would expose them to great books and constant discussion of ideas. We wanted them to have a personal relationship with the Lord, so we made plans on how to disciple them and reach their hearts. Clay and I both loved and performed music, and so we invested time in music lessons, according to the inclinations of our individual children. We wanted our home to feel like the best place in the world to them, so we planned activities, traditions, family feasts, games, and read-alouds.

If you do not have a plan or a philosophy, then you will try to fit your life into other people's plans. God has made each couple with the freedom to create their own family culture. The sooner you decide to embrace your own values, preferences, strengths, and weaknesses, the more you will become who God made you and your husband to be.

Of course, it requires faith to be yourself, to embrace your own ideals and family design. But living according to the voice of God's Spirit is always the way to freedom, joy, and fulfillment. Living by faith and cultivating your own purposes give you energy to pursue what is on your heart and to take your children along with you in the advancing of those ideals.

It is no wonder that our children are all musical, literary, passionate adventurers, and artists. That is quintessentially who the Clarksons are. We are not good at everything, but we embraced the talents and messages that God put on our hearts, and consequently, our children have grown up generally free from peer pressure. They have developed a love of pursuing their own dreams by faith, because that is what we modeled and taught.

So, sweet Sarah, and all of you precious moms who will read this, be yourself; be the best and most excellent and most righteous self you can be, but live in the freedom of God's call and design on your life. I love who you are and how God uses you. When you learn to hold His hand and walk by faith and obedience, you just might find yourself in the Hall of Faith of those who followed hard after Him and were allowed to tell a story of faith in their lifetimes.

Your Turn

Hebrews 7:19: "(For the Law made nothing perfect), and on the other hand there is a bringing in of a better hope, through which we draw near to God."

- Have you ever found yourself relying on law or formula to live your life? How so?

- Did you find that, as this verse says, that "Law made nothing perfect"?

- Confess to God the places in your life where you are relying on your own strength and formula instead of God's power.

READ HEBREWS 11:1–16.

- Count the different people in this passage. How many are there?

- Did their lives look the same? Was there a formula that meant that they turned out well?

- Each one of these people of faith was recognized as living an exceptional life, not because he followed a list of rules, but because he lived in the power of the Holy Spirit by faith. How does that affect you as a mother?

Something to Do

Find a piece of paper and write down the names of your children and husband. Under each of their names, write down their unique personalities and talents. Do you think that with such a diverse family, as each of us is bound to have, that one single formula could possibly allow them to live in the grace and power God has meant for us? Pray and ask God to help you to live an exceptional life with your family and children by faith, and not by formula.

For a video on chapter 3, scan this QR code with your smart phone or visit http://bit.ly/SoCwiA.

Dear Sally,

My sweet baby girl is so resistant to my training, and I feel like I'm losing my mind. I love her so much, but why won't she listen? I've tried different discipline and training techniques, but it seems like she defies them all. I'm trying to remember that she has a sin nature, just like I do, but it's wearing me down. How do I fight my own sin and hers?

Love, SM

Sweet One,

I have been thinking about you so often this week. No matter how hard you try, or how mature you become, you, your husband, and your children will always fall short of perfection. If you expect perfection, you are bound to become angry more often, with yourself and with your children. Children do not thrive with authoritarian, perfectionistic parenting, because they can never live up to perfection, and neither can you. If you want them to know the real message of Jesus, then you need to live out His life of gracious, forgiving love while becoming more mature in His ideals as you grow. If you accept the limitations of this fallen world within your own home, you will not be as tempted to depression or anger. As my son said to me, "Mom, just lighten up and be happy."

Hope you have a great day.

Fondly, Sally

CHAPTER 4

Oh Right, There's Sin

Sarah Mae

My two friends and I were sitting at the kitchen counter eating fresh strawberries from a local farmer's market and telling war stories. You know, stories about all the crazy things our kids had been doing recently. At times like this, we talk about what we do when our children back-talk, what training techniques seem to work well at what ages, what we do when we are sleep deprived, and on and on the stories and lamenting and encouragement go. We support each other and affirm each other and give counsel when needed. We love each other, and we cry and we laugh when we talk about life with little ones. This particular evening, much like our other times together, we found ourselves complaining a bit about the naughty things our children had done. And then my friend said something to the effect of, "If only I could cure my complaining problem! Guess we're not much different from our children!" We laughed and agreed, and the words went deep.

We are not much different from our little ones.

We sin. We complain. We rebel. We scream. We hurt. We are human, born with a sin disease swimming through our being, just like our babes. The Bible says, "Behold, I was brought forth in iniquity" (Psalm 51:5). How easy it is to forget that we live in a sin-infested world with sin-infested DNA.

As the undeniable reality of my own sin nature convicted me of how I view my children, I was reminded of something I had read in one of Sally's books. In *Mission of Motherhood*, she wrote about being frustrated with her children. She felt like her efforts weren't proving fruitful, and no matter what she did with her children or how many times she told them what to do, it wasn't working. Clay said to her, "Honey, at what age did you stop sinning? Because that's when our children will stop."

Wow. Is that a punch to the heart or what? It was for me. What a strong reminder that our children struggle just like we do. They have to fight the ugly in themselves, and it's no fun for any of us. They are operating out of what they know, and it's our job to civilize them (as my mother-in-law says). This means we need to offer them loads of grace and affirmation, so that they can be confident that we get it and we are on their team. I tell my children quite frequently, "Mommy needs help just like you. I need Jesus every day because I mess up, but He is gracious to love me and help, and He will help you too. We're in this together."

A Throne of Grace

My son has a passionate heart.

He is stubborn, but so authentic. He is honest and doesn't

mask how he feels. In the last chapter I told you that we went through a period of time when we were spanking him way too much. I want to share a little bit more of that time in our lives. After seeing that our intense discipline wasn't working, I began reading Sally's book *Seasons of a Mother's Heart*. There is a section on compassionate parenting, and it resonated in my soul. I showed it to my husband, and we agreed that perhaps we should work on understanding our son better, spending more time with him, giving him more affection, and training his heart, not just his actions. Sally doesn't say not to discipline, but she talks about the importance of understanding our children and paying attention to their worlds.

My husband and I began to listen to our son more, get close to him, and study him. One night I held him close as he was crying and saying over and over again that he was a "bad boy." No matter how many times I told him how much we loved him, he just kept saying that we didn't and that he was bad. I held his little tear-streaked face in my hands and said to him, "Son, you have a heart that wants to be bad." He started crying more, but I wasn't finished. "I also have a heart that wants to be bad. In fact, all of us do. But you know what? Jesus, God's Son, came to earth, and He had a good, perfect, beautiful heart, and He died so that we could have a heart like His. When we believe in Jesus, and we want to be like Him, He gives us a new, good heart! In fact, He not only gives us a heart that wants to follow Him, He put His very Spirit into ours, and it becomes one! Yes, we'll still do bad things sometimes, but He knows we want to be like Him, and He helps us. He loves you, buddy, and so do I, and because you know Him, you have a beautiful heart."

I believe the Holy Spirit made those words take root in my son. He got it. He understood that without God he has an ugly heart, but with God he has a beautiful heart. I'm telling you, God took up residence in my son, and my passionate boy prays with his whole heart when he cries out to God for help. I overhear him in his room sometimes, crying and asking God to help him. I check on him, and we talk, and we hug, and I love him well. He has the confidence to approach the throne of God. That is grace.

Hebrews 4:16 says, "Therefore let us draw near with confidence to the throne of grace, so that we may receive mercy and find grace to help in time of need." Do we allow our children to approach us with confidence, knowing we will receive them in a spirit of grace?

So often I get angry, and I yell and give them "hard face" looks and sigh when they want me again. I can be so ugly. Their little spirits are filled with much more grace than mine is. They are quick to forgive me and love me in spite of my bad behavior toward them. They teach me how to love well.

I want to be a safe place for my children. I want them to see that my arms are open and I love them no matter what they do. I want them to have confidence that their mama is on their team, whether they spill a glass of milk and break my favorite mug, or whether they scream at their sibling with harsh words, or whether they get out of bed fifty times, or whether they lie to me about something, I'm still on their team. I get them. I am them.

We are all just a work in progress.

Sally

At nineteen, my son Nathan was a passionate young man entering into adulthood, ready to have his "go" at the world. After praying for two years that God would open doors for him in the acting and music industry, through a miraculous string of events, God provided him with a scholarship to the New York Film Academy.

I was not thrilled at the idea of him moving to this big

metropolis at such an early age and was fearful of what evils and temptations lurked there to draw him away from his faith and commitment to biblical morality.

"But, Mom," he pleaded, "it would be demotivating for a soldier to do years of training and practice and never have an opportunity to engage in the battle to defend his country. I just want my opportunity to enter the fray after all these years you have invested in training us to be warriors for His kingdom."

And so we prayed about it and sent Nathan on a new and uncertain adventure, with the knowledge that though the world of New York City was filled with temptation and wickedness of all sorts, God also lived and worked in the Big Apple. From the day he arrived, we prayed him all the way through his schooling.

What kept Nathan strong through the many temptations and obstacles that came across his path was that his self-image had been developed as a warrior, and so he viewed his difficulties as opportunities to exercise his faith and take a stand for God. We taught him that this world is a dark place—the fallen place—but that as believers, we have light, strength, and messages of hope, and we could not wait to see how God would use him to bring those messages of righteousness to his generation.

Unfortunately, many moms have entered the battlefield of motherhood and are totally unprepared, untrained, and ill-equipped for the job. I know I was. And many have not understood that the home is a battlefield where sin and selfishness must be overcome, and that the taming, subduing, and civilizing of a home will be to a woman's honor.

I believe that if moms understood how strategic their roles were in this battle for the hearts and minds of the next generation, they would grow in excitement about this great job God created them to fulfill. For me, it changed my whole perspective to understand that this was a job for which I was designed before the fall, and that I played a key part in God's plan of redeeming this world back to Himself. Had I captured earlier the great call to train godly children, who would live righteously and invest in God's kingdom work, I would have been much more prepared and excited to face the challenges along the way.

Jesus said, "In the world you have tribulation" (John 16:33). He never promised that this world would be the perfect place, the place of ease and peace. The second law of thermodynamics gives us a clue to this world in which we are born. Basically, it states that everything is in a state of lessening energy and vitality. How true this is and was for my home and children.

We live in a fallen world that is in rebellion to God and His holiness. That means my children are self-centered, immature, and demanding; my husband has flaws and is vulnerable to his own weaknesses, temptations, and selfishness; and he is married to a woman whose focus is on herself, her own needs, dreams, and desires. This reality presupposes that a home and family naturally move toward chaos!

Many of us start our roles as mothers with a "Cinderella syndrome," thinking that life is going to magically work out happily ever after. I know I did, and boy was I in for a tough ride. Hollywood movies in today's world tend to create the illusion that life is romantic, things work themselves out in the end, and a happy home is easily won. But this is a lie, completely detached from the reality of our lives.

Wrong expectations produce anger and depression. Many women feel that they deserve to have it all; that they can work and have financial prosperity and time to themselves and a happy husband. More often than not, this leads to many days ended in disappointment and disillusionment.

If a mom also feels her children are out to get her and that her husband is intentionally insensitive to her needs, she will fume, steam, and yell, and act out her own self-centered demands and complaints that have little effect other than to strain her emotionally and physically. No amount of ranting or complaining can change the fact that we live in a fallen world. I wish I had known sooner that I needed to accept this reality, grow up, and determine to build up my strength little by little. It would have saved me so much emotional havoc in the long run.

And so I commission you, as you walk forward into your life as a mother, to look inside yourself and examine your heart attitude. We live in a fallen world, and there will be challenges and problems. Period. Jesus said, "In the world you have tribulation." He never promised that this world would be our heaven, or that we could ever make it so—after all, He was crucified here. However, there is a good ending to the story, knowing that Jesus has told us to "take courage, for I have overcome the world" (John 16:33).

This is the truth we must hold on to as we walk forward with confidence. Just as we were lost without Him, and in His mercy He saved us and granted us redemption, when we are lost as mothers, he wants to empower our lives and fill our homes with His presence. He desires to give us the strength to bring life into our homes and redeem them. God is a God of grace, and I have seen that He has done much more than my works could ever accomplish. He has wrought miracles in the lives of my children.

I have a memory of a friend asking me, "Why do you have so many miracles in your life?" Looking back now, I can see the answer to that question is that I need Jesus so much, and so often feel the need to allow Him to accomplish the things I could never do on my own. When I realized that He was with me and with my children, that He was my constant strength, and that He would help me conquer the battles in my home, it gave me the freedom to find rest in His abundant grace for me. We cannot be successful as moms alone, no matter how hard we try. But God with us is more than enough to build a wonderful legacy and influence. I offer to Him all that I am and all that I have, limitations included. Just like the little boy in the biblical parable of the loaves and the fishes, we submit our meager offering, and in God's hands it becomes enough.

Now, back to our soldier analogy. A young, inexperienced soldier would never be sent into a battle without extensive training and practice. He would also never go into battle alone or without a company of other soldiers around him and a general to give him guidance and instruction.

In our culture, we prepare women for their careers, for fashion, for romance and how to win a man, and most often in this modern time, for sex, and yet even our churches neglect to train and instruct young women on how to create a life-giving home. It can often feel overwhelming to surmount such seemingly unassailable walls. If you see the battle and feel like you are being overcome, know that it is a perfectly natural feeling. But it is a choice you must make to not dwell in guilt, and instead embrace God's helping hand. You must choose with God's help to be a victor, instead of a casualty.

In history, only those who act courageously and serve fearlessly become heroes. I have seen so many women give up on their ideals as moms, but I also see many older women who have conquered the building of a home, nurturing a godly legacy through the lives of their children. They embraced, in obedience to God, His call for them to build their home into a place of righteousness. It is an achievable goal, but it requires commitment, fortitude, and graceful endurance.

A Strategy for Winning This Battle

The first battle strategy starts with your heart attitude. You have to decide in your heart that you are God's girl. Proclaim it as truth in your life: "I am yours. I want to please you. I want you to be the one who gives me strength, wisdom, grace, and help, and I am willing to do whatever it takes to build my home for your kingdom."

Even Christian culture will often give women permission to see motherhood as a philosophy choice rather than as a high calling. However, for those who have said they will serve God, all success starts with the commitment inside to grow stronger, to be a conqueror, and to stand fast in this divine role.

Accept the Limitations

All soldiers are trained to expect and anticipate war, so they are not surprised when the battle starts. Moms need to understand that this is the reality of life with children in a fallen world. Getting angry and upset for children being selfish and demanding creates stress and havoc in the mind, emotions, and body of a woman. Prepare yourself for the battle and accept the limitations of your husband, children, and home—and of yourself. And then determine that you will, in time, subdue your home, overcome in the fight for the hearts of your children, and find God's joy and blessing through your obedience.

Your Turn

Romans 7:19–20: "For the good that I want, I do not do, but I practice the very evil that I do not want. But if I am doing the very thing I do not want, I am no longer the one doing it, but sin which dwells in me."

- Sin is the Murphy's Law of our attempts at righteousness. Do you identify with Paul in your desire to do good but inability to do it?

- Think of a recent situation when you wanted to do good (have a birthday party for your child, a romantic dinner with your husband, get the laundry done on time, etc.) and things went terribly awry. Can you see the evidence of our fallen world in your life?

Romans 8:1–4: "Therefore, there is now no condemnation for those who are in Christ Jesus. For the law of the Spirit of life in Christ Jesus has set you free from the law of sin and of death. For what the Law could not do, weak as it was through the flesh, God did: sending His own Son in the likeness of sinful flesh and as an offering for sin, He condemned sin in the flesh, so that the requirement of the Law might be fulfilled in us, who do not walk according to the flesh but according to the Spirit."

- We live in a world full of sin, but we are promised the Holy Spirit and forgiveness. What do you think it means to "walk according to the spirit"?

- Does God want you to live in condemnation of your sin?

- What does it mean that "Jesus has set you free from the law of sin and death"?

Something to Do

We live in a fallen world, so things will always tend toward disorder, children will always cry, and you will always sin, but God gives you grace and the Holy Spirit to make it through. When life tends toward disorder, go straight to God and ask Him for His grace to walk in the Holy Spirit.

For a video on chapter 4, scan this QR code with your smart phone or visit http://bit.ly/SoCFTb.

Section 2

Getting Real about Mama-hood

Dear Sally,

Lately it's been easier to put on the TV than put on being a good mother. I feel tired and lack motivation. I don't want to be depressed, and I don't want to lose these days with my children. I don't want the dark to win. How do I overcome these dark days? Did you ever struggle with depression?

Love, SM

Sweet Sarah,

I am so very sorry you have been feeling depressed lately. I truly understand and have been there many times myself. In nature, we see life and beauty in the spring and the appearance of death during winter. And yet this time of darkness is when the roots of all plants, trees, and flowers are growing deeper. And so I can see that it is in the most challenging and saddest of times when my soul grew the most, and I developed more compassion, humility, understanding, and wisdom. Just rest—rest in God's love; rest in this season, knowing it will not last forever. I wish you were next door, so I could bring you flowers and make you a meal. You must come visit me again soon!

Remember, I love you!

Sally

CHAPTER 5

When the Dark Invades

Sarah Mae

I was sitting in the small examination room waiting for the doctor, determined to figure out why I was so tired. What was wrong with me? Yes, I had little babes, two of them at that time, but I felt overly tired; the days were like molasses, and I was barely getting through. The doctor came in and sat down and began to ask me some questions. He asked me if my little ones still got up in the middle of the night. "Sometimes my son does." He proceeded to ask questions that clearly all pointed to the fact that I was a mom with little children and that's why I was so tired.

That's it.

That was the reason. Of course I felt silly and was convinced something was wrong with me, but everything else seemed fine.

So it was true, I was absolutely, genuinely exhausted because I had little children. In fact, apparently, it was normal.

I was normal. I didn't want to be normal! I wanted a solution, a drug, a diagnosis that said, "You poor dear, you have this, and THAT is why you are so tired. Here's what we can do to help." No such luck for me. When you're a mama of littles, you are just tired and have to weather it. There is no cure or solution. So there I was, stuck with the reality that I would have to leave the doctor's office without my problem fixed. This was my life for the foreseeable future.

I remember so many nights waking up and singing the song in my head from the band Switchfoot with the lyrics, "This is your life . . ." I just resigned myself to the fact that I would be tired most of the time. And I was. And I still wanted a cure, but the fact was that sleepless nights and caring for babes and taking care of the home and trying to meet my husband's needs all just made me tired. Even when my children started sleeping through the night, I would wake up thinking I heard someone crying. It was madness! I think a mama can't help but be on alert; it's something in the way God weaved a woman, I suppose.

Trying to function through our days being down-to-the-bone tired can make any mama feel desperate. I felt like such a failure when I would be so tired that I just wanted to put on a movie for the babes, so I could grab a few more minutes of sleep. How was I supposed to be homeschooling when I felt too tired and wanted to find something else for the kids to do? Even reading to my children seemed an almost impossible task.

When I set out to write this book, I was exhausted. My third babe was two and was still getting up every night, sometimes more than once. My son, who was four, also had a habit of coming in my room to kiss me in the middle of the night and then go back to his bed (yes, it was very sweet, but it did interrupt my sleep). I was a wreck in the mornings and would cry out to God, "How am I supposed to be a mother when I'm so tired?!" I was feeling desperate. But now, as I'm writing this chapter, my daughter will turn three, and my son is turning five, and they sleep through the night most of the time. I have better perspective now and can see that the season of sleepless nights is almost gone, and I won't be as tired. But even in the midst of the tiredness, I can look at my children and see that they are loved, well taken care of, secure, happy, healthy children. They didn't suffer as terribly as I assumed they would because there were days when Mama barely did more than kiss and feed them. And those kisses and that food, it was enough. We all got through by His grace. And you, mama, with the sleepless nights and the ache to have energy, you're going to get through as well. Maybe you have many children and your season of tiredness won't come to an end in any foreseeable future. It must be very hard for you, and I hope that you have help, but I know that God is good and faithful. He cares for every little bit of your tiredness, and He knows how you're feeling. You hang in there, mama. I'm praying for you right now. You are blessed.

A Word on Depression

Here is something I wrote when I was struggling with depression:

> Mama never said there'd be days like this. My whole body feels like it's rebelling against me. How can you be a mom on days like this, let alone a sane human being? Life is hard when you're emotionally inside out. No matter how great your circumstances are or how much you love your children . . . or Jesus, life is hard when you feel the darkness invade your spirit. And you can't just pull your boot straps up, no matter how cute they are.

I haven't slipped into depression since last year. And it is a slipping, a slow slipping in which you don't notice you've been falling into the dark until you wake up one morning and getting out of bed seems to be the most difficult task of your day. That's when you know. You look back and you see the signs. You've isolated yourself. You've thought about how much you've failed your children. Your motivation has dwindled. You're comparing yourself to others again, and of course, you see yourself as the one that's no good. "Why bother, I'll just mess up again" has become a common phrase from your lips. These are the signs. And the bed that knows your apathy is the bed that you can't leave. This is depression.

I fall in and out of that dark place, and when I'm in it, it feels like solitary confinement. I feel alone and crazy and think, *Why can't I just get it together?* But when the dark lifts and the light is there again, I think, *Why did I let myself go to that place? I'm a happy person!* It's like how everything at night is amplified, serious, immediate. The daylight comes and everything seems okay, and you think, *Life isn't so bad, after all.* It's the battle between the light and the dark, and it's as old as time. And make no mistake, it is a battle.

Right now, I'm in a season of light, and it feels like the dark could never penetrate my soul. I'm happy and content, and I feel like I am in a place of victory. I've chosen since the new year to overcome, to not be a victim of depression. Does this mean I won't ever get depressed again? I don't think so. What it means is that right now, I'm choosing to fight the dark; I'm taking steps to stay in the light. I will overcome. I will not be a victim. I will keep my eyes on Jesus and the hope that there is always a new day to start fresh. It is not by my effort, this overcoming; it is by trusting Jesus with all the crevices of my heart—the dark and the light.

Are you struggling with depression? I wish I had some perfect answer. I can only offer what has helped me: making a very conscious choice to be in the Word, eating the bread of life every day, and recognizing that I am not my bad days. I will not let the dark tell me who I am. I will give only God the authority to tell me who I am. I will choose to be a participant in my own life; I will not let this life or my dark days control me.

I am resolved.

Resolved to walk with my God on the good and the bad days. Resolved to trust in who He says I am, righteous and perfect (2 Corinthians 5:21; Hebrews 10:14).

And it's helping tremendously. I pray that you, too, will find a resolve. It's not a cure, but there's a whole lot of hope in it.

Sally

I was hiding in my second-story bedroom, sinking down into my old beloved recliner that had held so many of my secrets: feelings of despair, hidden dreams, and closet thoughts that no one ever perceived or heard. The sun was setting over the myriad pines out my window, and the darkness slowly spreading across the cold of the snowy day seemed to reflect my own heart's reality. It was deep, creeping darkness, ten tons of weight resting on top of my mind, so that breathing became difficult, and I felt a palpable frigidness of heart.

The grim reality of those feelings was all too familiar to me, and knowing this process from having gone through it many times previously in my life, I carefully avoided panic or despair and instead immediately went to my secret place, where I knew God would meet me. Psalm 27:5 says, "For in the day of trouble He will conceal me in His tabernacle; in the secret place of His tent He will hide me; He will lift me up on a rock."

As a little girl, my daughter Joy had a secret closet, a tiny space in the corner of my room where we hung a lantern and placed a pile of beanie babies, with which she would play and play for hours. It was her "secret" place. People would come and go in our home with stress and discussions and needs, and Joy would hide, away from all the prying eyes, certain we would take care of life while she rested and played.

And so, when I read this verse that says God will hide me in the secret place, it immediately reminded me of Joy taking shelter in her closet when any trouble came her way. God is the one who would meet trouble when it knocked at my door. I could hide away, find rest and peace, and put all of my darkness, fears, resentments, and exhaustion into the file drawers of His heavenly office and leave the responsibility to Him.

I have learned over the years that depression and bone-tired weariness is a part of the battle. As I have so often remembered, Jesus said, "In this world you have tribulation." Battle comes as no surprise, or shouldn't if we are reading the Bible and take it at its word. But the next admonition is equally as true, and far more powerful when walking through our burdens: "So take courage."

Hiding away in God's goodness and protection is an act of the will, choosing to turn my heart away from the dark toward the light. And so, when met once again with the darkness of fear and anxiety, my heart immediately brought to mind the words of my commitment: "I will not allow depression to have control over my life to rule me. With God's grace and the power of His Holy Spirit who rests in me, I will, by faith, mount up over this new barrage of circumstances that has threatened me, and let God's grace and faithfulness take me through to the other side."

I have no desire to negate the present and overwhelming struggle so many have with depression, but I have learned that in every situation, when I understand my relationship with God, I also see clearly that He is beside me and loves me with an everlasting love, far outlasting any darkness I feel right now. "If God is for me, who can be against me?" By faith, we put one foot in front of the other.

In my own walk I have learned to implement a strategy of wisdom that has consistently allowed me to make my way through these periods of struggle to the light on the other side.

Assess Your Needs

For me, making a specific plan to face the giant of depression always lessens its impact and shortens its duration. I have a little mental checklist that I review:

1. Do I need sleep? I need to do whatever it takes to restore physically.
2. Have I been reading my Bible? Even if it is putting an app on my phone with a voice I can listen to while still in bed in the mornings or at night, I need to hear from the God who walks through these valleys with me.
3. Do I feel alone? I need to call someone who is a spiritually engaging friend, one who loves God, loves me, and whom I can completely trust. I will meet that person for coffee or lunch to share my heart and to ask for prayer.
4. Am I watching my health? Exercise is a stress reducer and helps happy hormones to develop. I have developed the habit of walking and hiking.
5. How can I get help? Is there someone who can help me clean my home? Do I have a friend I can ask to keep my kids, so I can have a little time away?
6. What do I need to invest in the joy factor of my life? Am I creating spaces of beauty for my own soul—candles, music, fresh flowers, and other such life-giving things? Perhaps it's

as simple as going to a movie with my husband or friend, or buying a new scarf.

There are so many different personal issues to consider, but I have found that sometimes when we choose to look away from the mountains of anxiety and stress that have endangered our souls, and instead attend to our souls, we will find that the depression will quickly dissipate.

Discipline Your Mind

So many scriptures tell us to be vigilant to guard our minds and hearts, so that we do not believe lies and give in to fearful and despairing thoughts. We know that Satan loves to accuse God's character. The first thing he did to tempt Adam and Eve was to suggest to them that God was lying to them about the Tree of Life, that God did not have their best in mind, and that there was an easier way.

Once we go down the road of providing for our own needs instead of waiting for God to provide, we are in dangerous territory, just as Adam and Eve were when they made a choice to disregard God, to forget His goodness, and to act apart from His will.

God has an unimaginable amount of love for us, His children. It is a truth that Satan will always try to suggest is a lie. Once you start going down that road of feeling invisible and thinking that God doesn't care, the natural consequence is despair—the dark hole where faith cannot exist. God says to worship Him with all our mind. There will be so many times when we will ask God what we already think and feel: "Do you really love me? Do you see my pain? Do you know my needs? Do you understand my broken heart? Will you ever answer my prayers?"

Feelings and dark thoughts in the midst of battle are not wrong or sinful. Even so, what we choose to do with those thoughts is imperative. If we are to worship God, we must tell Him how we are feeling and confess the feelings and thoughts of our hearts, just as we would to our own loving parents or friends. Then we must say, as Jesus did through the prophetic Psalm 22 of His own feelings on the cross, "Yet You are holy." We can proclaim, "And because I am choosing to believe that you are loving and providential, and that you do care, I will choose to worship you with my mind. I will take captive every dark or anxious thought I have and give it to you. I will choose to cling to what the Bible tells me is true."

Philippians 4:8 has been a place of refuge for me to go in such times: "Whatever is true, whatever is honorable, whatever is right, whatever is pure, whatever is lovely, whatever is of good repute, if there is any excellence and if anything worthy of praise, dwell on these things."

Learn to Wait with Grace

Understanding that God is God and embracing Him even in the dark places, can become the story of my greatest faith. When all else seems hopeless, and yet I still turn to hope, it brings great honor to God and renders Satan utterly powerless. I often think back to one of my daughter Joy's favorite sayings: "It is better to light a candle than to curse the darkness."

Surveying the many years of my own journey with the Lord, I see so clearly how the dark places are those in which God was shaping my very soul and conforming me to Christ's image. He was stretching my heart to understand pain in such a way that I could exercise compassion for those who would need it in their own journey of faith.

As a young woman, I idealistically dedicated my life to God and said, "I will be your girl. I will follow you, obey you, and love you all the days of my life, and I will believe in you always." My heart was innocent and committed when I said this, but I didn't know that I was but a toddler in my faith. I did not understand that God would bear with my tantrums and shaking of my fist, and then in time faithfully train me, so that I could become mature enough to actually be used by Him. Hebrews 12:11 promises, "All discipline for the moment seems not to be joyful, but sorrowful; yet to those who have been trained by it, afterwards it yields the peaceful fruit of righteousness."

Our heavenly Father often does not rescue us from our messes because He has high standards and hopes for us, desiring to shape our souls into the image of Christ. He allows us to interface with the difficulties this world presents, with the intention to ultimately use them for our good. He uses this world as a training ground, so that we may become strong and righteous. In order to defeat the darkness and emerge once again into the light, we must submit our will to His and know that our precious, loving Father will, in His time, work all things together for our own good.

Your Turn

Read Psalm 91.

- When you are feeling trapped by your fear or despair, where is the first place you turn for refuge?

- Do you view Jesus as your protector and provider?

Psalm 27:1: "The Lord is my light and my salvation; whom shall I fear? The Lord is the defense of my life; whom shall I dread?"

- What are the things in your life you look to for your "light and salvation" besides God?

Something to Do

Find some time to go to your favorite cafe or coffee shop, or any place that fills up your soul. Ask a trusted friend to join you, and share your heart struggles and desires openly with her. Make sure someone you trust knows what's going on in your life.

For a video on chapter 5, scan this QR code with your smart phone or visit http://bit.ly/XaYvh2.

Dear Sally,

I am so undisciplined! Trying to train my children and myself is very difficult, and so often I botch it up. I know I need routines in our life, and I know my children should have consistent responsibilities, but I can't even get myself to be consistent. Do you have any suggestions on how I can become a more self-disciplined person in the midst of teaching my children to be self-disciplined?

Love, SM

Hi Sarah,

If only you knew how untrained and unprepared I was for this task. I had never even washed clothes when I moved away from my home! Housework has never, ever been my strength, and dirty dishes in the sink will always make my heart drop. Yet I focused more on the atmosphere of my home, the rhythms of keeping it going, and in time my capacity to work became stronger and I didn't feel quite so overwhelmed. Also, if you train your children to be involved in the chores of the house with you, you will find that you have your own built-in housekeepers. As with anything else, practicing working and building housekeeping skills takes time, but remember that your home is a place of life and it is not supposed to look like a House Beautiful *cover. Get help from time to time and be sure to get a break away from home. If I ever inherit a lot of money, I promise I will hire you and me full-time housekeepers.*

Be blessed today!

Sally

CHAPTER 6
Lack of Training

Sarah Mae

I remember thinking once how I wished I had been disciplined as a child, because then I would be a disciplined person now. I ache for the training I never had.

As I've told you, my mom was a wounded woman (aren't we all?) who, I think, was brought up in such a regimented, cold family that she must have vowed that she would be completely opposite of her parents. She would be authentic, honest, and raw. And she was those things. She never edited when she talked. As a teenager, I loved the honesty my mom gave me. She treated me like I was her age. Which was a problem because I wasn't her age; I was much too young for her open talk and loose boundaries.

She was not a model of self-discipline, and I received no discipline from her.

Then there was my dad, the man who hung the moon in my world. My dad, way too gentle and protective of me to ever physically hurt me, spanked me one day. I can't remember what I did, but he basically gave me one pat on the behind while I was standing up, which didn't hurt in the least. I have no recollection of ever being disciplined after that, but for some reason I remember that funny little spanking memory. I think it warmed my heart, knowing that my dad was trying to be a good disciplinarian, but he was just too gentle to actually go through with the physical punishment. In fact, after that, my dad won me over by the calm in his voice. One stern word of disappointment from my father was enough to give me a remorseful heart.

But unfortunately, it wasn't enough to discipline me.

I honestly can't remember one time in my life when I was disciplined . . . not one. I was threatened with grounding and the like, but it never came to pass. Any obedience that was given was purely out of a child's natural submission to parental authority.

I know you might be thinking, *You're lucky you were never disciplined!* On the surface I can see how that would seem like a good thing, but, friends, it was not good. It left me wildly out-of-control without any anchors to put down.

Lack of discipline and a lack of training go together. In order to be trained in something, you must become disciplined. I was never disciplined or taught the art of discipline, and therefore I completely lacked any serious training in what pretty much everyone should have training in: homemaking. It's one thing to watch your parents do the dishes; it's another thing entirely to be shown how to do them and then given the responsibility of doing them every day, day in and day out for years. Discipline. Training.

And now that I have to train my own children, I yearn for the training I never had. Now I have to train myself and my children; it's the blind leading the blind!

Serious Lack of Experience

I had never changed a diaper until I was out of college and working at a crisis-pregnancy clinic. I facilitated a group of single moms who needed help and support, and it was during one of those groups that I offered to change a baby's diaper. It's so funny, looking back now, because once I took the baby and laid him on the couch, I had no idea what to do. It all seemed simple enough, but I was still nervous. I managed to get that baby all cleaned up and changed (it really isn't rocket science), but the fact that in twenty-three years of my life I hadn't changed a diaper is a sad commentary on the lack of domestic training I received. I bet many of you can relate.

In addition to not knowing how to change a diaper, I also did not know how to do laundry. Until I moved in with my mom when I was in eighth grade, I had never laid a hand on my own laundry (seriously!), and had no clue how to do it. My mother wasn't exactly a laundry connoisseur, and she certainly wasn't into training in the domestic arts, so it was up to me to figure it out. I put my clothes in a laundry basket and headed for the very large laundry room and took my first steps toward a washer. Wait, which one was the washer, anyway? I stepped over piles and piles of clothes (I kid you not, you could not see even an inch of the floor), and I walked to the machine. I opened what I hoped was the washer and began to read the directions that were on the lid. I can't remember how things turned out that day, but it is still not an area I have mastered. To this day, I don't separate lights and darks, and if you asked me what starch looks like or how to use it, I would stare at you with a blank face. My husband has banished me from doing his laundry (I tend to shrink clothes). Clearly, I still need to learn a few things!

I always fall back on the crutch that I'm not training our children well because I was never taught the art of discipline and hard work. Too bad I have a will and a healthy body and mind that give me no excuse for choosing not to train and discipline my children . . . and myself.

The truth is, I am at a disadvantage compared to someone who was brought up with training and discipline, but so are many others! I was also never taught how to become a good writer, but here I am writing anyway, learning as I go and making plenty of mistakes along the way. I was never taught how to cook, but I manage to feed my family every night. We sit down and eat together, something my family never did. There are plenty of things I was never taught that I choose to learn and implement now because they are important to me.

And training and disciplining myself and my children are very important to me. I let our lives slide for too long using the excuse, "I wasn't trained." Again, while there is some validity to that excuse, it has an expiration date: the day you decide to make a change.

You make that decision and then you resolve to persevere. You will mess up more times than you succeed at first, but that doesn't mean you stop. It means you keep going, pushing into your "why" and remembering what you wished you would have had. You can make it different for your children. You can give them a better start than perhaps you had.

You have the choice.

You won't change by yourself, but over time, as the Spirit intercedes, you will mature. Remember, He's with you, always working for your good.

Sally

I can remember having heard a story, that I later learned was a fable, about Marie Antoinette, the queen of France, who grew up in great wealth and opulence, just prior to the French revolution. She was raised in an Austrian palace as a child and had servants who attended her in every detail of her cushy life. She never had to work or pay for anything, and every need was fulfilled without a cost to her. When she moved to France to become queen, she naturally had no concept of the reality of the devastation of her subjects in France, most of whom lived in abject hunger and poverty, barely scraping out miserable lives.

The tale says that she looked out from her playhouse gate, an extravagant locale that had been built for herself and her children in a lavish garden, and saw in the far corner of the street beyond the castle a thin, dirty child begging for bread. In a rush of pity, she cried out, "Let us give the child cake to eat!"

There was nothing about her life that had prepared her for the real world, so she was considered to be an empty-headed, shallow woman. I suppose I must admit that I felt a little like her when I first interfaced with housekeeping. I had never done it, never been trained for it, and had no idea of the magnitude of it. In my mind, I was simply going to play house with my children like I did when I was a little girl. To the average bystander, I might have been considered lazy, disorganized, and weak in my ability to keep up with basic household chores. The reality of the matter is that I had never really been trained.

Of course, I had washed a few dishes in my time, and done a little dusting here and there, but most of my life, things were more or less done for me. I had never washed a load of clothes until college. I had no experience in what it would take for me to keep children fed, groceries shopped for, clothes washed, organization in place, and beauty kept and created, let alone meeting my children's needs in the midst of it all. I didn't have an inkling of what awaited me as a mother! I had never given thought to putting systems of housekeeping into place before. I didn't know what cleansers to buy at the store, and I was not efficient in any way doing the work of homemaking.

As a young mother, anger would nearly engulf my overwhelmed heart when the sink would become full again and the clothes would pile up, and I would think my family had it out for me. I took all the messes personally. *Really? Another mess?* I would have moments of near-resentment for my children and my husband, just for wanting to eat and live in my home. The piles of laundry, the messes of clutter scattered throughout the house, and the smudges and dirty floors, not to mention all my high ideals for shaping my children's souls that were cast aside during a crisis of cleanliness—housework definitely overwhelmed me.

Clay, my husband, is one of the most naturally organized and neat men I have ever known. I am quite sure he did not expect me to be so inept at keeping our home in order. To this day, it is still by far the hardest area for me! Housekeeping is relentless—it never stops and piles up day after day. If I could have my way, I would rather be eating cake in a playhouse.

Feeling condemned for not getting it all done can be an immediate source of depression for many women. We all assume that others can do it better than we can, and also assume it must come naturally to some women. As I have surveyed the many women I have known in every stage of life, it seems to me that housework is always an overwhelming challenge, regardless of personality.

Cultivate an Attitude of Contentment

We all know the story of Martha and Mary. Surely we are all able to sympathize with Martha's exasperated frustration: "Do you not care that I am doing all of the work?" If you ever had any doubt, you can be assured that this is an age-old problem.

It has taken me many long years to realize that letting grumpiness become a habit when doing housework was useless, and more often than not, only served to make me angrier. God has taught me that I need to decide to accept the work as a normal part of life and not struggle against it. The first step in dealing with the frustration of housework is to understand that it is never going to go away.

A second step is closely related—don't measure your success in life by your ability or inability to do housework efficiently. I hear so many stories from young women whose mothers were neurotic about keeping a well-organized and orderly home, and as adults they feel guilty if they ever make a mess. Your relationship with your children and their ability to enjoy the comfort of your home are gifts you can give your family by choosing to accept and appreciate the limitations of a full and lively house. Solomon understood it rather well: "Where no oxen are, the manger clean" (Proverbs 14:4).

When I realized that I had six oxen in my stall all the time, it gave me peace knowing that the messes that reflected the six people in my home were a part of having all of us together!

Copy Wise Women

A wise woman copies wise women. I learned from others. I would ask them questions, observe their homes, and then apply their wisdom in my own home. I also had to decide what fit my home and personality and what was unrealistic. For me, in general, relationships trump work. Of course work must be done on a regular basis. Yet, because my priority in life is discipleship and winning my children's hearts for Christ by showing them His love, I have often had to drop what I was "accomplishing" in order to listen to their heart or settle a fuss and train them to choose character or to make peace or to write out a verse. It has helped me to see other women in their own approach, and see how they weigh their own values against housekeeping. I am then able to synthesize that gained knowledge into my own personal approach.

Learn also from women who have written down their thoughts. Read some books on cleaning. Look at magazine articles that show how to keep up with small children in a house. Practice routines and rhythms so that your work is kept up in a regular fashion so that things do not go to total disarray.

Make a Plan

Making a plan and putting my chores into a calendar helped me to begin to get a handle on my many tasks as a mother. Someone once gave me the sage advice to "clean as I go"; it has been a faithful and helpful approach. I practiced making my bed when I rolled out of it in the morning. I began putting away clothes the moment I took them off. I would put a dish in the dishwasher as soon as I was finished with it. All of these simple things made my day easier to handle.

I gradually learned how to bring some fun into the process. I would put on loud, rhythmic music while we were all cleaning up the house or doing the dishes. It became a time of shared fellowship, and many memories were made as all of us would sing and dance while doing chores together.

We also developed the practice of "Five-sies." This meant that on most days, around five in the afternoon, I would set a timer for fifteen minutes, put on some music, give out assignments to the kids, and say, "If we can get the house mostly straightened in fifteen minutes, we will share a 'Five-sies' snack." When we were done cleaning, I would light a candle and put out a tray of cheese sticks, some sliced fruit, a few roasted nuts, or some whole grain crackers, and we would spend ten minutes of civility together. I made an anchor of it in my day in which I could get the main areas (kitchen, den, dining room) straightened up, into a semblance of order so that when Clay walked in, all appeared as somewhat neat and together. And it goes without saying that everything had a place to go—books on bookshelves or under the coffee table, toys in lidded boxes, dishes in the dishwasher, pots and pans in their appropriate cupboard. I felt good having order in the rooms Clay would see when he got home.

Work to Serve Yourself and Accept Your Limitations

I have realized over the course of my life as a mother that I have some strong areas in which I excel, some weak areas that I find difficult, and certain kinds of work that I flat-out dislike with every bone in my body. To make it through housekeeping, you will need to custom-fit your plan to yourself. Simplify. Take a break. Hire some help once in a while if it's within your budget. You are an important link in helping the rest of your family feel you are creating an environment of peace and grace.

The more I grew in this area, the better my self-image grew. Though I had never been taught how to be efficient, I established foundations and structures, and with God's grace made it through. I now take comfort in the knowledge that my children consider my home the best place to be; not because it is immaculate, but because it is a safe haven of meals shared, love expressed, and relationships cherished. Such work is accomplishable and will give joyful life to you and your family.

Your Turn

James 1:5: "But if any of you lacks wisdom, let him ask of God, who gives to all generously and without reproach, and it will be given to him."

- When you feel overwhelmed and underprepared for your life as a mother, are you willing to turn to God first, and accept His loving offer to "give to all generously"?

- Are there attitudes and frustrations to which you default, rather than accepting the help of a heavenly parent in your own role as a mother?

Hebrews 12:1–2: "Therefore, since we have so great a cloud of witnesses surrounding us, let us also lay aside every encumbrance and the sin which so easily entangles us, and let us run with endurance the race that is set before us, fixing our eyes on Jesus, the author and perfecter of faith, who for the joy set before Him endured the cross, despising the shame, and has sat down at the right hand of the throne of God."

- Do you have a clear sight on what your final goal is in your work as a mother?

- Are you allowing yourself to get distracted by the hectic and messy nature of life, or are you keeping your eyes straight ahead on Jesus?

Something to Do

Write down a couple of goals in your journal, things you desire to see come to fruition. Keep them short and within the range of weekly accomplishment. When you have finished, pray over them and entrust them to God, knowing Him to be a good Father who wants to help you.

For a video on chapter 6, scan this QR code with your smart phone or visit http://bit.ly/P0igGa.

Dear Sally,

I am so selfish! Every day I see it in myself more and more. I don't want to be selfish, and sometimes I'm just tired. I'm sure you must have struggled with selfishness. How did you push past it? How did you choose every morning that you would put away your own selfish desires and choose your children?

Love, SM

My sweet friend,

Selfishness is the very root of sin. I didn't even know I was selfish until I had children. But being self-absorbed never really made anyone happy. Putting aside my own needs and choosing to serve my family has helped me grow more in my walk with the Lord than anything else I have ever done. I wish someone had told me early in my marriage and mothering that I was lazy and I needed to decide to learn to work harder. Nothing excellent is ever accomplished by being lazy or selfish. Once I got over my pity party and decided that I was willing to do whatever it takes to build excellence into my life and home, my motivation increased and my vision for what I could accomplish stretched, and as I look back, I am now amazed at my capacity to work so hard and to get so much done. The end result is that my labor has been rewarded and I have felt the joy of building something of great worth. So develop a willing heart and become the best mom you can be by getting rid of the destructive attitude that we all have—that of selfishness—and decide to be an overcomer! I believe in you!

Sending love!

Sally

CHAPTER 7

Sacrifice in the Mundane (On Selfishness)

Sarah Mae

Days are long and mundane. Every need, every ask, every complaint feels like a burden. I'm angry and tired and I don't want to take care of my children. I love them, but I just want to hide away and do my own thing and have everyone leave me alone. I want quiet and time and long, hot baths with no interruptions. I want to do what I want to do.

I'm selfish and don't I know it.

"Mommy, will you play dragons with me?"

"Mommy, will you do a craft with me?"

"Mommy, will you sit with me and watch this movie?"

Most of the time, I just want to run away and hide. Motherhood is too hard for me.

I am selfish to my core.

I'd rather write or read or do nothing but drink my coffee and stare out the window enjoying the peacefulness of the falling snowflakes. I don't want to spend twenty minutes bundling my children up and go outside in the cold and tell them not to throw snowballs at each other's faces and then rush them back inside because no one went to the bathroom first. I want to be where it's warm and quiet. I don't want to deal with the mess that comes after the snow: the wet floor, the gobs of damp clothes and coats and boots.

In theory, I love the idea of my children frolicking in the snow and coming in for hot chocolate and an old episode of *Lassie.* But something in the last couple of years has changed. I've gotten tired, and the thrill of watching my children light up at the glories of a new-fallen snow has been shadowed by my tired spirit. I guess the truth is that I liked watching my children explore when it was new for me too. When I had one little one and everything was a grand experience for the both of us. Now, after three babies, the new is gone and I'm back to my ugly root: self.

Selfishness is an ugly, life-sucking disease that infests our very DNA. I think I have an extra dose of it.

I long for the thrill of something new. I ache for the joy I once had when I had my first baby. I ache for the hearts of my children who have been put in front of a TV screen, so that I don't have to entertain them. I ache for my ugly heart, and how desperately I want it to be beautiful and humble like that of my Father.

This selfish blood that burns me with guilt and threatens the souls of my children, this selfishness cannot live. I need to bleed it and be filled new with the blood of the One who laid down His very life for those He created. This is the sacrifice we are all called to make: "Greater love has no one than this, that one lay down his life for his friends" (John 15:13).

Pushing into Sacrifice

"God is opposed to the proud, but gives grace to the humble."

James 4:6

The opposite of humility is pride. And it is my own pride that keeps me from doing the hard thing and giving up myself for the sake of my children.

Pride, that ugly beast that convinces us we are better, above, more important. If we didn't believe these things to be true we'd easily lay aside our own agendas and offer our lives to our babes in order to give them the time and training and actual love that they need. You and I, we love our children to the core of our beings. We would die for them. But for some reason, we have a hard time putting away our books, or our computers, or our crafts in order to serve them, train them, encourage them, and fill their souls with life. Every day.

What is so hard about playing ponies? Or sitting and doing a craft? I think it's two-fold. One is that it's boring to play with little children sometimes. Sitting on the floor playing ponies and trying to drum up conversation between Star Song and Rainbow Dash gets old really fast. Two, we know that if we sit down to do that craft, our two-year-old is going to jump in, make a mess, fuss, upset the older ones, and everything is going to go south fast. We've done this before, so we know.

Choosing to enter into the mundane with our children, who see playing ponies as anything but ordinary, is a sacrifice of love. Choosing to enter into a project that will probably turn into a training session is also a sacrifice of love. We will have to choose patience and kindness over frustration and giving up. We'll have to choose to take time to train and teach and perhaps discipline. The choosing to engage means choosing to do the hard work of loving through our actions.

It means taking the time to cultivate the souls of our children. Cultivating has much to do with playing ponies, doing crafts, getting wet socks in the snow, watching a movie when you have something else you want to do, staying in their bedrooms a little longer even though you're exhausted . . . I believe these acts of love and sacrifice pay off in a child's heart. Because it shows them we care, and we want to be a part of their worlds. I think it also shows them the Father's love. Our Jesus was meek and patient and said, "Let the children alone, and do not hinder them from coming to Me" (Matthew 19:14).

My children are still little, and I know I have time to change my course, to choose love, to sacrifice in order to care for them well. I have time.

Are your children still in the home with you? You have time! Ask Jesus to help you, to mature you, to teach you how to begin laying down whatever it is that has your attention and choose to offer yourself to the souls in your care. You will be glad you are able to one day look back and say, "I was intentional; I was faithful; I chose my children." You will reap what you sow, and you can reap so many precious gifts from those efforts when they become adults, marry, and have children of their own. Put in the work now.

We take our children into the sanctuary with us on Sunday mornings to worship together as a family. My husband and I made a commitment to bring our children—ages three and five at the time—in with us even though we knew it would not only be difficult, but we would be one of the only (if not the only) families in our church doing this. Most children went to Sunday school.

The first time we brought our children in, the people around us thought we were crazy, and we thought we were crazy too! Our three-year-old son had to be taken out of the service a few times, and my daughter had a hard time sitting in her chair (of course!). But we committed to the philosophy that our family should worship together and that our children would be a part of the church and not in a sub-group of the church, and so we persevered with resolve and grace. After several weeks, our children were used to sitting in the sanctuary with us, and now, nearly two years later, it is a joy to have them with us. They know how to be quiet, and even though they still get fidgety (they are just kiddos!), they listen and ask us questions about the sermon. Looking back, it was hard work to get our children to sit quietly with us during the service, but the work has paid off, and we are enjoying the fruit of worshipping with our children.

If we put in the hard work now, we have a great possibility of seeing the fruit later. If you want to do the hard work, there are two things I can recommend as being beneficial: commit to being faithful, and then walk out your commitment by faith.

Find Time for Yourself

As soon as the door shut, I went upstairs and prepared to write; I had the house to myself, and I was so excited for this quiet time that was all mine in this space. I went into the bathroom and pulled my hair back to wash my face. I don't wash my face as often as I should, but today I did. I splashed the warm water over my skin, taking the time to gently clean it thoroughly. I took care of myself, and I did everything slowly and purposefully. Dressed and ready for my coffee, I glided into the living room and straightened up the pillows on my sofa knowing that they would actually stay straight for a few hours and look pretty. I cleaned up my living room, lit a candle, took the dishes to the sink, and got my comfy chair ready. I made my coffee, put in my caramel creamer, and started thinking about what I wanted for breakfast. I had time to think! I decided to make myself an egg sandwich: egg over easy, salt, minced onions, bacon, and cheese on a toasted English muffin. Yum! I sank myself into my comfy white chair and prepared to get on with writing. It was going to be a great morning. I was getting a soul-filling.

Day in and day out we give to our children, and it's a privilege to do so. I'm thankful for the opportunity to pour into my children, but when we choose to give the best of ourselves to them, we will need a break, or we will break. We'll get desperate.

I remember the days when I hardly had any breaks, and I thought I was going to go crazy. I would wake up only to long to be able to fall back asleep because of my exhaustion and knowing that today would be like every other day: long, hard, monotonous (I hadn't learned yet about choosing to bring beauty and life into my and my children's lives). I needed a break—an extended time to be put back together again. I needed God, space, nurturing, time, and cupcakes. With sprinkles.

I needed that dreadful "me" time.

I say "dreadful" because "me" time has selfish connotations, and I didn't want to be a selfish woman. Thankfully, my perspective has changed (and I'm a saner woman). I think it's more selfish to go crazy and then not be fully alive for your children.

The bottom line? Find a way to get out. Find your happy place, your soul-filling space, and go. If you don't have a husband, ask a friend or someone at church (whom you trust and know well enough to have watch your children) if you can work something out where you get a consistent time away. It's so important.

And if you can't find the time, hold on tight to the hope that your season for rest will come. For a couple of years I couldn't get time away consistantly, and that is one of the main reasons I felt so desperate. Please know that I understand if you are in that place. But God has been so faithful, and somehow I got through, and now I am able to get consistent time to recharge. And it's good. I'm healthier for it. I'm praying right now that you will be able to find rest, refreshment, and hope.

Sally

The temperature had been below thirty-two degrees for over a month straight, and claustrophobia had set in deeply. I felt conflicted inside, because although I deeply loved my wonderful little baby girl, I became increasingly restless the more I stayed cooped up at home. Living in Austria as a missionary family was sometimes fun and fulfilling, but also often very lonely. Clay went to work in the city, and I would often spend up to twelve hours without speaking a word to an adult. None of the women I knew had a little baby. So many of my days were spent alone, playing "baby play" with my sweet daughter, feeding her, changing her, waiting for her to go to sleep or wake up.

Eventually I made a decision to get out of the house so as not to go stir crazy. I bundled up Sarah, wrapping her little body from head to foot in a jump suit, little boots, a scarf, and a woolen cap, and set out on the cobblestone streets to find some adventure and entertainment. At the tram stop, I struggled on with my stroller and finally found a seat, cuddling Sarah into my lap. I placed her looking out the window, so that we could both see the sights of downtown Vienna. In one final transition, we climbed out at the nearest subway stop and boarded a fast train that sped to the inner circle of Vienna.

Baby Sarah seemed to love the fast ride and giggled all the way to the end stop in front of the famous Hotel Sacher, an elegant five-star locale in the very center of downtown Vienna. I decided to enter the hotel as though I were a guest there. Tiny sparkling little shops lined the perimeter of the luminous hotel lobby, with a little café in the atrium. People smiled at me, pointed to Sarah, and made gestures of "sweet baby" in a variety of different German phrases. I strolled up and down in front of the delightful shops, let Sarah toddle and run about with her fat little legs in the looming lobby, and had a nice cup of coffee, sharing my biscuit with her. She was delighted, and I had filled my emotional cup by getting away from my lonely apartment to an interesting and soul-enriching environment. I remember it as a lovely afternoon, and it became a paradigm for me for the rest of my mothering years.

One of the marks of a godly woman is that she takes responsibility for her soul's need for joy and delight. A woman is a conductor, who leads the orchestra of her surroundings in the songs and music of her life. God is a God of creativity and dimension, and so He is pleased when we co-create beauty in our own realm, through the power of His Spirit.

It was a profound realization when I understood that I could become an artist with my very life. I was responsible to do what I needed to do to last on this long road of motherhood. There was some point in my life when I accepted that no one else was going to take responsibility for me, and if I didn't take care of myself, my soul would die a slow death by exhaustion, boredom, loneliness, and mediocrity.

You Are Who You Are for a Reason

God gave me my personality. I am one who loves adventure and travel. I'm a social person who loves friends. I am a reader, thinker, and have an artist sort of soul. God does not admonish us to sacrifice our personalities in order to please Him. Instead, He calls us to uphold His ideals and design. He wanted me to grow fully into the person He created me to be, in order to give to my children what they needed. The more I have learned to cultivate a life that is interesting to me, the more interesting my home has become to my children.

Don't Try to Fulfill Everyone Else's Expectations

Returning to a common theme in this book, there are so many voices and opinions about motherhood and parenting today. You can become neurotic if you try to follow every bit of advice. It will kill your heart for motherhood if you compare yourself to everyone else's ideals. You have to be yourself and live within the limitations of your personality and needs as a woman.

Some moms have become so frenetic about being a mom that they have forgotten how to be a human being. To be clear, I am not talking about sacrificing my children on the altar of my pleasure. But it seems to me that God has given all of us generous leeway in conducting our own symphony of life, and in cultivating our family culture according to our own strengths and weaknesses.

There is almost too much advice available about motherhood for moms who don't have a strong self-image of themselves as mothers and don't know what to do. Many sweet moms I know break under the pile of guilt for not "keeping up with the Joneses." I quickly found that I would inevitably fail any attempt to fit into the box of any "ghosts" of expectations, and so at a fairly early age, I sought to find freedom in Christ to do and be myself within the ideals of His biblical design. There were always rules to make me question myself:

"The best time to meet with God is in the early hours of the morning—if you don't study the Bible then, you will miss out on His voice of greeting."

"A real mom keeps all of the insides of her drawers organized."

"A real mom sews; after all, the Proverbs 31 woman did."

"A real mom corrects every single disobedient action of her children."

"A real mom doesn't work or spend time away from her children."

There are so many laws, rules, and formulas out there that can pile up burdens of guilt on any mom. I think this is why Jesus was so harsh in His condemnation of the Pharisees' actions and attitudes. Living by performance always kills our souls because none of us are perfect mothers, and we will fail in some areas, so we need to live by God's approval and mercy to feel His grace.

After my happy venturing out in Vienna, I began to seek out time to go away to plan and dream about the goals of my life. Often, Clay would stay at home on Saturday mornings to make waffles for the kids or take them out, just so I could snatch a little time.

What did I love that I wanted to pass on to my children? Books, art, music, ideas, the Bible, beauty, hospitality, feasts, travel, relationships, ministry, spiritual concepts, the love of outdoors and nature, writing, playing an instrument, drama, missions . . . and the list goes on.

Because I was aware of what I loved, I was able to build some of those joys into my interaction with my children, as an anchor that gave both me and my children pleasure. If a mom is passionate about what she loves, her children will learn to have passion and joy in their own lives, following the leadership of their mom.

Daily I placed my kids around me on our little couch and read excitedly from a children's Bible. I would cuddle them up and tell them just how much God and I adored them, and the practice became an anchor in our lives.

I would buy flowers every week to put in a tiny vase on our table, light candles every night, and put beautiful music on, so that they would learn to love beauty. I needed beauty for my own soul, and by modeling it in my life, my children came to love beauty as well. Their little souls were shaped by such experiences, and as adults they take joy in embracing many of the same habits.

If we were caught inside for too long a time, I would whisk them all out to the car, and we would drive into the mountains on an adventure, listening to a book on tape and enjoying little snacks along the way. We all delighted in such outings. My soul needed it and their souls were shaped by it.

Having read that books and stories were the best ways to shape intellectual prowess and intelligence in the minds of children, I would take all of us to the library to pick piles of books—colorful ones, adventurous ones, biographies, silly ones, fairy tales, and the like, and let each child have their own book to check out, even as toddlers. I would spend hours each week reading stories with my kids, discussing their meanings and being captivated by their grandeur. Along the way my soul would be filled and theirs would be shaped by great literature.

You see, God wants you to be alive and share in that life with your children. He wants to help you develop a foundation of joy, imagination, and beauty in the lives you share together.

Experiences like those described above, as with any other part of life, don't just happen. You must have a plan. What kind of home do you want to live in? How can you craft a home and a schedule that is interesting for you and your children? In taking responsibility for being a conductor of the music of your and your family's life, you will find joy and fulfillment, and, as I did with my sweet kids, eventually find that you have developed your own best friends out of your own children, who have learned to love what you love.

Your Turn

John 13:12–14: "So when He had washed their feet, and taken His garments and reclined at the table again, He said to them, 'Do you know what I have done to you? You call me Teacher and Lord; and you are right, for so I am. If I then, the Lord and the Teacher, washed your feet, you also ought to wash one another's feet.'"

- Jesus, a king who lowered Himself to the most humble posture in the presence of His disciples, is our example of how to have a servant's heart. Are you following His example to forgo your own rights for the sake of those around you?

- When you serve others, do you do it for your own sake, from a heart of self-righteousness, or do you keep your eyes on Jesus, who gave His all for His disciples out of a heart of love and submission to His Father?

John 15:13: "Greater love has no one than this, that one lay down his life for his friends."

- Jesus emphasized self-sacrifice as the greatest love. Are you willing to give up all your rights for the sake of blessing those around you?

- Are there any particularly important rights that are difficult for you to give over to God?

Something to Do

Take each of your children out to a fun restaurant or favorite haunt for some one-on-one time. Encourage them and speak particularly into their lives, letting them know you value them and are willing to give up a little time to bless them.

For a video on chapter 7, scan this QR code with your smart phone or visit http://bit.ly/SoDgV3.

Dear Sally,

When my life feels overwhelming, I escape to the Internet. I tuck myself in between social media channels and try to find life there when mine feels drained. I know that is not good, and I'm ashamed to admit it. I know life can only be found in the Life-giver, but sometimes I choose the Internet instead. It's an easy escape from the mundane days. Did you ever have escapes? How did you choose reality instead?

Love, SM

My dear one,

It is irrational to think we are supposed to do this very difficult job of mothering without the support of others, with no time off, and not eventually want some kind of a break. I finally learned that if I was going to last in this long journey, I needed to take responsibility to fill my own heart and life, so that I could keep going. Addictions and idolatry come from seeking to fill the holes in our lives with unhealthy substitutes for what we really need. So please get help, call me, take a break, do something you enjoy if you find yourself being tempted to become addicted or practicing coping skills that are not healthy. Learn to put your finger on your deep felt need and then write down how this need can be met in healthy ways. Your needs are important, and a godly woman learns to recognize them and then fill her life so that she can stay strong and vibrant over the long haul.

Sending you flowers today to remind you that you are loved.

Sally

CHAPTER 8

Escaping

Sarah Mae

I can remember the first time I got what you might call a high from the Internet. I don't know how old my children were, but I know that I hadn't had my third child yet, so they were probably one and two years old. A very popular blogger was hosting a forum on building a better blog—growing your audience, earning money, that sort of thing. I ended up staying on that forum all day long until my husband got home. It was the first time I'd ever been on the computer all day. I'd always been very intentional about not using the computer too much when my children were awake, but for some reason on that day I was drawn in and hooked. By the time my husband came home, my day had gone by so fast I could hardly believe it. You see, normally my days went by like molasses, I was so bored. Of course, I thought to myself, *I will never do that again.* But it was still a great day, and as I look back, I think that is exactly when it started for me, the addiction to being online. Being online made life interesting; it was my escape from the mundane.

I really believe that because we do not have the community support families used to have, young mothers with little children are more and more drawn into alternate realities, to places that are big escapes from the mundane life. It is so easy to get lured into an addiction through false reality. I know some of you struggle with Internet addiction. I know that some of you struggle with emotional affairs or perhaps a full-blown one. I know some of you struggle with the addiction of uppers to get you through your days. There are other addictions, but they all have the same root—you're probably lonely, and life is dull. You don't have support or community. I'm not trying to make excuses; I'm just saying that I get it because I have been in the same place and I'm like you. I'm home with little children, and I am learning more and more to lean into God. I have to because I am in this life race for the long haul. And what keeps me going is the fact that I want to be a woman of integrity. I don't want to look back in fifteen or twenty years and regret my choices during these days just because they were long and hard. I want to look back and know that I was an intentional mother doing everything I could to nurture the souls of my children. They need me; they need me in their reality.

If you're struggling with some sort of addiction or strong temptation, make a commitment before God and do everything you can to run away from the temptation, and get help from someone if you need it. I think the most painful part of turning from an addiction or an alternative reality is that if we're really honest with ourselves, and with God, we know we like the sin or the false reality. We've got to get real. It's helpful to have a friend or husband or a counselor to confess to. We need to be able to acknowledge that we like our addiction, it feels good, it's easier than life, and we want to keep doing it. We've got to say these things out loud, so they aren't hidden in the dark where the enemy traps. Speak the truth before your God; He knows it anyway. We need to commit to praying that God will help us turn from our addictions and temptations; we need to ask God to help us understand the root of what is going on in our hearts. We need a resolve. And when you feel like you can't go on, you've got to call a friend and ask her to pray over you, and speak truth and grace over your life. Get on your knees before God and tell Him you're sorry and ask for His help—we can't fight without Him.

I have found God to be extremely faithful when we cry out with a pure heart. A pure heart isn't one that is unmarred by sin; having purity of heart means you want to do the right thing, crying out to God and His truth and for help. I believe that God will help us. I believe that honesty with ourselves and before God is powerful. If we want to be women of integrity, we've got to be women who think about the future and its consequences. If we don't, we could end up like the woman in Lamentations 1:9: "She did not consider her future. Therefore she has fallen astonishingly."

A Confession

Sometimes I avoid my children.

The last few days I've been in a cleaning mood, which my husband says only happens about twelve times a year (I think he's being generous). I've organized my two bookshelves, the buffet in the dining room, and the top of my piano. I've kept my kitchen (mostly) clean. I've swept and straightened pillows and dusted. And when my daughter asks if we can do a craft, I tell her I have to clean my bedroom.

Clearly, I'm not winning the parent-of-the-year award today.

I'm not entirely sure why I'm doing all this avoiding. I love my babes; I love who they are and how God weaved them. I'm pretty certain spending time with my children doing what they would like to do is something I need to get better at. But there is a deeper revelation that God is surfacing for me.

I have a problem giving myself to my children; laying down my life, so to speak, for them. And it's an ugly revelation. I'm trying to escape from my children, from my life. That root of selfishness is sunk in deep, and I'm asking God to pull it out and throw it away. I'm still in the process, working out this selfishness, but I want to be present for my life, every season of it. I'm asking Jesus to help me experience the new life He has already given inside me. I don't want an escape; I want to trust Jesus with the life He has given me.

Sally

One dark afternoon, when the temperature had been below zero for twenty-two days in a row, I thought I would blow a gasket. I loved and was committed to my children, but I didn't feel love that day. I just wanted out. I just wanted to escape.

I found a babysitter on the spur of the moment and couldn't get out of my house fast enough. I felt so dark inside that I didn't feel very motherly. I didn't think I could take one more hour of the fusses and the cries of my baby, who simply refused to go to sleep. I wanted more—friends, fun, and time to myself.

Of course the feelings that followed were of guilt—deep guilt that I, as a Christian mom, who was committed to this role, could feel such negative thoughts about my children and my role as a mom. I remember thinking that something must be wrong with me. However, looking back with eyes far more nuanced, I see that I was totally unaware of the truth that feelings do not equate worth.

Getting married when I was twenty-nine meant that I had many years of singleness. I had traveled many places, worked as a missionary, and become accustomed to a European lifestyle. I had immensely enjoyed all my adventures and the many interesting people I met and made friends with along the way.

It is during the times when we are most overwhelmed with feelings of inadequacy and depression that we are most vulnerable to a snare. One of the most potentially destructive forces in a woman's life is when she begins to look for fulfillment in something or someone else—a fantasy relationship, drinking, addiction to attention. Secret sins hide in the hearts of so many women I have met over the years. The most common letters I. receive are from women who believe they have failed because they feel lured by those traps.

Yet we read in Scripture, "No temptation has overtaken you but such as is common to man; and God is faithful, who will not allow you to be tempted beyond what you are able, but with the temptation will provide the way of escape also, so that you will be able to endure it" (1 Corinthians 10:13).

Think about that—there is no temptation that has come your way that is not common, regular, normal in the lives of everyone you know. It is not a sin to be tempted. All of us are tempted. And all of us are weak and vulnerable. We must recognize this, so that we can look to others for help.

Many women I know feel so very guilty and inadequate for having negative feelings or for being tempted by different issues that they suppress their desire to seek the grace of their heavenly

Father and lose themselves in a sea of guilt. Satan loves it when we hide because we become prisoners to our temptations and the ways we have fallen.

Motherhood is such a high calling that it should come as no surprise for it to be fraught with stress, difficulties, and challenge. Motherhood in an unsupportive culture becomes even more difficult. The loneliness, boredom, and isolation of women alone in their homes compound the issue even further. And now, with the Internet, television, telephones, and computers, there are a myriad of new ways to distract and lead a mom away from her center.

One of the biggest problems with isolation from others is that there is no accountability—no one knows what you are doing with your time or the imaginations of your heart. No one is there to warn you or to help you in your soul struggles.

However, we must understand that many of the things that seemingly promise ultimate fulfillment and affirmation are just dead holes that steal away the heart, time, and emotions of a mom left to herself. Before a problem becomes chronic, it is immensely important to find someone who can help us be accountable. What we sow, we will indeed reap. If we sow loneliness without accountability or friendship, we will reap a loss of perspective of the danger of our idols and temptations.

"This isn't so bad for me. I need this to keep going. Everyone needs a little help or pleasure once in a while." Whether it is drugs, alcohol, an addiction to the Internet, romance novels, television, or vain imaginations about someone else outside of your marriage, addictions are all the same—they promise life outside of the only One who can give life, and ultimately deliver death.

Most of us receive permission in our culture to do whatever we please—"You deserve a break today." "You deserve time alone."

"You are giving so much to everyone else; you have to have this to keep yourself happy." "Everyone makes a mistake once in a while." Whatever line is used to justify a habit or an addiction or a temptation, in the end it is exactly that: an excuse for compromising our lives and looking to something else to fulfill our needs.

The amazing truth of it all is that God really wants us to be fulfilled and joyful. He wants us to find real fulfillment in real people, real work, real accomplishments, and not in things that substitute for life. As believers, we need to champion each other's lives and struggles, and love and support one another so that each of us will be given the opportunity to end our journeys well.

No one else can take responsibility for yourself but you. A hard lesson I have learned is that a mature woman must take responsibility for her own happiness. If we are feeling lonely, then we need to figure out ways to find like-minded friends with whom we can cultivate healthy relationships. If we are weary, we need to build rest into our schedule. If we feel empty, then we need to figure out a way to bring pleasure into our lives. If we are failing to thrive and falling under the weight of addiction or immorality, we must learn to recognize these issues and get help.

If someone was physically ill, we would not fault them for going to a hospital, and so when women are emotionally or spiritually ill or despondent, we need to help them find the support and accountability they need. If you are the one struggling, please, please talk to someone about your feelings, addictions, or temptations. There is nothing worse than hiding them; they will only grow more pronounced and will bring even more heartbreak when they inevitably come to light. Find someone to whom you can entrust yourself—perhaps an older woman, or a pastor or counselor at church. Get help. Do not hold this burden on your own.

Be Preemptive About Your Needs

If you are a mom who knows a friend who is going through some of these issues, decide ahead of time to come alongside her, but be careful not to condemn your friend, and in so doing drive her away. It is sad that many Christian moms are so focused on their rules and standards that they have forgotten that Jesus looked out on the multitudes and felt compassion because they were like sheep without a shepherd.

Christians should not shoot the wounded with pharisaical attitudes. Instead, just as Jesus was a redeemer who took initiative to reach out to the lost and pull them up into life, so we, in our gratitude for Him coming to our aid and for showing His generous and unconditional love, must come alongside each other and "bear one another's burdens, and thereby fulfill the law of Christ" (Galatians 6:2).

I remember a time when I was quite depressed and overwhelmed. Not even realizing the weight of burdens I was carrying, I lived in the darkness of soul worries. I had bills to pay, a child who was chronically ill, another child with OCD and a heart that wanted to rebel in his teen years, a little girl who wanted a normal "play with me, Mommy" life, a husband who was depressed, and four national conferences ahead where I was supposed to be spiritual and have all the answers.

Seeking to be as faithful as possible, I was only finding the energy to put one foot in front of the other, one day at a time. Then out of the blue, a friend left a card in my mailbox. The note read, "I know you are weary to the bone and I don't know how to help you—but I have scheduled a massage for you to at least give you one hour to rest and relax."

Though thankful, I hardly knew how to take the time off from my busy schedule. I went almost purely from some subconscious obedience to the spa. Yet, in one hour, just having someone spend time on me, releasing tension from my body and giving me a chance to rest, restored me more than I could have imagined. The love offering of my friend started to melt the layer of ice that had developed on my heart, and a small crack opened to let light shine through. I began to mount up energy, hope, restoration, and focus for the days ahead.

Yes, I did make it through this difficult season and saw God's faithfulness, but it was because my friend chose to be the loving hands of God to help me begin to imagine making it through my struggles with grace. We all need a community of friends to help us, and sometimes that means you have to start the friendship! God will help you fill in the empty spaces as you entrust yourself to those around you, and seek healing and grace.

Your Turn

Galatians 6:7–9: "Do not be deceived, God is not mocked; for whatever a man sows, this he will also reap. For the one who sows to his own flesh will from the flesh reap corruption, but the one who sows to the Spirit will from the Spirit reap eternal life. Let us not lost heart in doing good, for in due time we will reap if we do not grow weary."

- If you take a good look at your life, what are you sowing?
- What will you reap in ten years from the choices you are making today?
- What is the good you need to keep on doing no matter what?

Matthew 9:36: "Seeing the people, He felt compassion for them, because they were distressed and dispirited like sheep without a shepherd."

- God sees into the very deepest of our needs and discouragements with complete love and compassion. In what areas of your life do you need to know the compassion of Jesus?
- Do you believe He can shepherd you out of these hard places?

Something to Do

Take some quiet time away with God and make two lists. On the first, list the good and beautiful things you want to do, things in which you need renewed encouragement and life. On the other, list the areas of your life in which you are weary and failing, or are tempted to sow wrongly. Commit both lists to God, picturing Him as the Shepherd who knows your needs.

For a video on chapter 8, scan this QR code with your smart phone or visit http://bit.ly/TEHaIb.

Dear Sally,

My house is a mess, and I'm so overwhelmed. I just wish I had someone to help me clean it. I clean one room, and ten minutes later, it's wrecked again. And the laundry? Please tell me you have some sort of system for laundry! When did your children begin to do their own laundry? How much cleaning did you require of them? Tell me I'm not crazy to want help and that it's okay to have it! I feel so guilty because I feel like as the keeper of my home, I need to do everything here. But I'm drowning, Sally. What do I do?

Love, SM

Dear Sarah,

My best advice to you is to get a housekeeper! If only I could! Over the years I have learned that making this area of my life as simple as possible has helped me to better keep up with the tasks. Make a plan to do the regular chores and then engage all of your family, including your husband, in doing them on a regular basis. The more it becomes a part of everyone's expectations to get the work done as you go, the less often the house will overwhelm you. Even now, when I do get behind and get overwhelmed, I put on loud music, call in everyone for a thirty-minute "taming of our house," and then we all work together to get it back to a semblance of order. Also, accept the fact that if you are alive, there will be messes. But also, do some pleasurable things to make it suit your soul. When I add a vase of flowers or a seasonal decoration and make my home a place that pleases my heart, I am more inclined to want it to be orderly. The place is connected to my heart pleasure in the living here every day.

Go be an artist today, sweet one. I am off to do so myself!

Sally

CHAPTER 9

Taming the Beast of Housework

Sarah Mae

Can we please all just a take a moment to recognize the second law of thermodynamics?

Yes, that one, the one Sally talked about earlier. The law that states that everything is heading toward death and decay, one otherwise known as the curse pronounced on Adam and Eve in Genesis 2. We are fighting against the fact that dust settles, things get old and wear, and our bodies are just . . . tired. Death and decay.

Let's face it. Not only do we have to change diapers, feed babies, wake up completely groggy—sometimes running into our dresser and stubbing our toes as we try to reach our little one before she wakes up the others—but we have to give them clean clothes to wear, clean dishes to eat from, and a safe, swept floor to play on. To leave housework out of the desperate discussion is to ignore the reality that housework is half the battle! If we all had maids, or servants as the Proverbs 31 woman had, taking care of our children would be easier (not easy, but easier). A great burden would be lifted if we had help in the housework department, but since many of us don't have the help, we must learn to tame the beast of housework. And I do mean tame it, not create a showplace.

Know Your Strengths and Your Weaknesses

I'm starting this section with strengths, because we all do the proverbial kick to ourselves when it comes to the things we're not good at. It's easy to focus on our weaknesses. We drown in them, we make excuses about them, we get depressed over them, we make vows because of them, and we oftentimes let them break our resolve. We give up, thinking we'll never change. Well, we may never change the DNA we were weaved with, but we can change our minds about how we view ourselves in lieu of our weaknesses, and we can choose to focus on our strengths.

I am very weak at keeping tidy. I don't like doing dishes, laundry, washing windows, mopping floors, or any other mundane cleaning activity. But I wrote an entire book about cleaning. And you know what the heart of that book is about? It's not really about cleaning; it's about loving others well. My weakness may be scrubbing toilets, but I have strength in my heart that tells me that sometimes scrubbing a toilet is a way to love my family and myself well. Mind you, if I can have someone clean that toilet for me, bring it on. I am not above help, but I do derive satisfaction in bringing life and beauty to my home through a warm, clean (not sterile), life-giving atmosphere. When you come into my home, it may not be pristine, but you will find a cozy place to sit, some pretty things to heighten your senses, a vanilla fragrance in the air, and a prop-your-feet-up-and-stay-awhile environment. It won't be perfect, but it will be maintained because I care about making you feel loved through your senses in my domain. I also want my children and my husband to have this same feeling.

> *"Our house is clean enough to be healthy, and dirty enough to be happy."*
>
> —Author Unknown

Recognize the Mundane and Buy Pink Cleaning Gloves

If you are not the cleaning type, then you are going to have to recognize that cleaning is a necessary, mundane task, and you may just need to buy yourself some pink glittery scrubbing gloves and get on with the work!

The bottom line with cleaning is that we have to find what works for us. Set a timer, make a list, dangle a reward in front of yourself, make it a game (and involve your little ones), play music, but do something! And know why you're doing it.

The "why" is powerful. My "why" is so that I can love people well.

When I take care of my domain, giving it life and filling it with beauty and comfort and warmth, I am saying to myself, my family, and others, "I love you! Come on in, put your feet up, stay awhile. You are welcome here." I am not all about having a house that is more like a museum than a home. I want things clean and orderly (where are my keys again?), but I'm not looking for anything close to perfection. I couldn't if I tried, really, because my personality just won't stand for it. But I will choose to give labor to creating a welcoming home where people feel loved and at peace.

My encouragement to you? Find your "why" and get on with it.

And if you have the means, there is nothing wrong with hiring some help. If I could, I would hire maids for all my friends who have little children.

Sally

I ladled cold raspberry soup into little crystal bowls I found at Goodwill and topped it off with a delicious swirl of whipped cream. It brought a satisfied smile to my face. Candles were lit, music wafted across the room, and I was ready for all of our friends to come to our yearly Christmas tea at our home. My girls invited their closest friends, and I invited mine. It was a tradition formed long ago, which has continued to this present day, rife with joy-filled memories.

With made-up faces, bejeweled necks, and girly attire, we all launched into the celebration of our friendship and heart fellowship. However, at some point the conversation took an unexpected twist. I had asked the girls to tell all of us what they thought their own lives would look like in ten years.

"To be honest," one girl shared shyly, "I don't want to have very many kids like my parents did, because my mom is always worn out and grumpy."

"Yeah, I agree. The way my mom acts about housework, always complaining, fussing, and running about lecturing us just makes us feel guilty, so whatever my future holds, it will not involve a house full of kids and messes—it just seems too hard."

I gently tried to stir the comments in another direction, but the point had been made. When a mom complains and fusses as a regular way of life, it will inevitably go into the hearts of her children with great force.

No child wants a mom who complains and whines. No child

of such a mother will ever say, "My mom tried her best, but she couldn't help being lazy, grumpy, or a nag. It was just who she was." They most certainly will say, "I always felt guilty in my home because my mom was never happy, and she complained all the time. It was such a relief to leave." I know this because of the countless adult women who said the above statement to me. We can't get away with anything with children. They are keen and attentive, and they will eventually grow up to tell the story of their home.

On the flip side of that sentiment, I have come to see that a happy mom is a real gift to her children. A good attitude about work makes her children feel that she is glad that she is a mom and that she is thankful for her children. She communicates to them that even with a full workload, she is fulfilled and content.

I have struggled with housework my whole life. But the reality I have come to understand is that children and husbands are going to want to eat three meals a day, every day, and want to wear relatively clean clothes. All children want to see their home as the best place to be, and whether they are aware of it or not, your actions and attitudes in the home will form that opinion more than anything else. Having said that, I want to pose three major areas I have been honing over the course of my life as a mother, which have helped me to minimize my own stress and tame the beast bit by bit over the years.

Making a Marriage with the Nature of the Beast

At some point, if you want to find relative happiness and peace in your home, you must accept the limitations of your children and husband, who will regularly make messes. This is a part of life for every family, in every corner of the earth. There is no magical book, formula, or set of rules that will ever change the workload associated with a home and family.

The attitude I adopt every day has the potential to affect the whole demeanor of my home. As the saying goes, if mama ain't happy, ain't no one happy. Consequently, a vital part of maturing is deciding to be content through obedience, and to cultivate a spirit of joy by choice. Feelings go up and down; it is how we choose to respond to feelings that will determine our ultimate attitude.

I have learned that my capacity to be mature and work hard is far more expansive than I ever knew. The more children I added, and the more workload in ministry and life that came my way, the more I found room to grow and work harder than I'd ever thought before. Learn to be faithful and choose to be content. It is a practice that over time will help you be stronger and more able than you ever thought.

Make a Plan

There was a point when I had three children five years old and under, and it seemed that all I was doing was reacting to the spills, fusses, and messes of life. I was allowing my children to control the direction of my day, rather than moving forward into my day according to my own regulations. I eventually realized that regular anchors in my day would bring us back to order and help us all to work at having a tidy home.

I looked for natural anchors, places in my schedule that would metaphorically hold my family to the dock of life. For instance, bedtimes and meal times were things that needed to happen at the same time every day. I also knew that I needed to start including my little ones in the rhythm of work so that they would learn to expect it as a part of life. I wanted to engender a self-image of being a responsible person in their home and to take initiative for their own messes and chores. Teaching habits like this takes time, of course, but when children know what to expect, they are much more likely to comply.

Every morning, after breakfast and devotions, we assigned rotating roles to each of our children for washing the dishes, cleaning off the countertops, and emptying the dishwasher. I made sure to make this a regular ritual before setting forth into anything else in the day. Often, as the kids got older, I would put on fast-paced, energetic music during chore time to make it more fun. I have a lot of fond memories of loud singing, dancing, and silly antics. And each afternoon I would stop what I was doing at a set time and tell each of the kids that I wanted to make our home beautiful for Daddy, so that he would be happy to be home.

A directly connected anchor to that is bedtime routine. The kids would put up any last toys, brush their teeth, put on pajamas, and then, if they were ready and in bed by a set time, we promised to read to them before lights-out.

Of course these things are never exact; but by creating these anchors, no matter how life had fallen apart during the day, I could always come back to my center because my children knew what to expect. Even to this day, they will straighten the living areas around five o'clock, so that when we all gather for the night, we have a great environment to share.

There were also times when we would devote a day to getting everything back to spick-and-span. Nothing would depress me more than mounds of laundry or piles of messes, and even with daily routines, things pile up. When it got to the point where our everyday habits were insufficient to keep up with the messes (and this happens in every home, no matter how organized), we would stop everything else and get our house back to normal.

Of course, even beyond that, I can remember occasions when I was pushed beyond my limits of usefulness into overwhelmed nonproductiveness. In anticipation of such times, I would save my pennies, cut back on other luxuries of our monthly budget, and pay for someone to come in and help me get back to normal. Having someone else work from time to time was a grace to me, especially when our children got older and we traveled more often. It was my own way to figure out my own housework puzzle. Find out for yourself what the most confounding things in your own world are, and come up with a workable schedule, with solutions that suit your own hours and days.

Create a Haven—For Your Own Sense of Well-Being

Picture yourself as an artist. Crafting beauty, color, aromas, tastes, fun and humor, love, and comfort—these are all aspects of creating a life-giving environment in your home. The point of keeping a home is not to be perfectionistic or neurotic about cleanliness and order but to create a life of balance that brings joy to your world and those around you.

When you give consideration to your own personality and desires in the crafting of your home, you will be happier with the results along the way. Even now, as I am sitting in my living room, I can see points of beauty and order everywhere. Books, pictures, a tea tray and candles, my Pandora music wafting in the background, all these things give pleasure and scope to my soul, even when I am in the midst of countless stresses and deadlines. You must take the time to think about how to construct an environment that brings you the pleasure of your own crafting.

A sweet young mom friend of mine said that she saved $200 to deck out her living room. She asked a girlfriend to accompany her, and they explored a thrift shop and an economy store, and came back with colorful pillows, framed pictures, candles, and a vase with dried flowers to spread around the room. Afterward, she remarked that she felt like she was in a totally different world.

I learned from my mother to always light candles at the

dinner table and put music on every evening, whether we had a piece of toast or banquet fare for our dinner. It calmed down the children and soothed all of our souls. Even when my children were very little, they were drawn to the beauty of flickering candles and rich music. Bringing them pleasure also brought me fulfillment.

Learning to think in such a life-giving way ended up being a real motivator for me. The mundane is a heaviness that compounds stress to make life feel even more unmanageable. Adding color and interest into the tasks of my life significantly diminishes that weight of stress and refills my soul to keep going. Listening to a book on tape while folding laundry or playing loud music while cleaning the kitchen makes the chores so much more enjoyable.

The reality is that a family, eating, creating dirty dishes, playing, making messes, and having fun simply generates lots and lots of work. The constant stream of work will never really stop flowing; it will only change and morph over time. Your home will never be perfect, but accepting housework challenges as a part of a normal life and embracing them as part of a regular rhythm will allow you to enjoy the people in your home. When you do, your children have the potential to remember home as a place of harmony and positivity.

Your Turn

PROVERBS 31:17–18: "She girds herself with strength and makes her arms strong. She senses that her gain is good; her lamp does not go out at night."

- In what specific areas of housework and home do you need to "gird yourself with strength"?

- What "good gain" do you want to reap with your work?

- What goals do you need to set to accomplish this?

Proverbs 9:1–6: "Wisdom has built her house, she has hewn out her seven pillars; she has prepared her food, she has mixed her wine; she has also set her table; she has sent out her maidens, she calls from the tops of the heights of the city: 'Whoever is naive, let him turn in here!' To him who lacks understanding she says, 'Come, eat of my food and drink of the wine I have mixed. Forsake your folly and live, and proceed in the way of understanding.'"

- What sort of atmosphere are you creating for your children in your home?

- Are they called to goodness by the home and life you are shaping for them?

- What influence does the atmosphere in your home, the work you do, and the attitude you have toward that work communicate to your children?

Something to Do

Choose one or two specific areas of housework in which you want to improve: healthier meals, a better system for laundry, or simply the creation of a daily schedule. Then make some specific goals and outline a plan for how you can "gird yourself with strength" to make it happen. Consider what wisdom or grace your work in these areas communicates to your family.

For a video on chapter 9, scan this QR code with your smart phone or visit http://bit.ly/RfHxMl.

SECTION 3
The Redeeming

Dear Sally,

I'm ready to start over, to take on life and motherhood from a fresh perspective. I want to overcome and lean into Jesus where I'm weak. I want to put anchors in place and plan to steady my course. But I'm a little lost on how to begin. Any words of wisdom for me?

Love, SM

Sweet Sarah,

I have every confidence that as you create a new plan and work toward its fulfillment, you will find new affirmation for yourself deep within. Written deeply into our being is a gratification for subduing or beautifying life. Women are such great civilizers, and to look on the product of your own making will create more joy than you can imagine. Make your plan suited especially to your tastes, your personality, and your wishes, and you will be more likely to own the work that is to be done. Remember that the consequences of mothering well are truly great. You have this opportunity to ingrain love, righteousness, and faith into the very depths of your children's souls. Such potential influence is in your hands. God's Spirit will give wind to your wings and He will bless you as you embrace these ideals for His glory.

Love you, my sweet friend,
Sally

CHAPTER 10

Figuring It Out New

Sarah Mae

I have no foundation in homemaking or baby-raising. I only babysat maybe three or four times, and one of those times I was late and was never called back. I never wanted to babysit because I didn't like it; I found it boring. Entertaining other people's children was not my idea of a good time. But I also never developed an interest in it because no one ever cultivated that desire in me. I had never learned how to put away my own selfishness and reach out and help others. I wish I had a mother who taught me the value in caring for children, one who taught me about raising children, feeding them, changing them, nurturing them, training them, etc. When I had my own, I was starting from scratch, and no matter how many books I read on baby-raising, they couldn't fill the place that hands-on training would have given me.

When I brought my first little baby home from the hospital, a little girl, I was not prepared for the long journey. It's kind of like marriage and the wedding; we spend so much time preparing for the wedding and hardly any time learning and preparing for the long-haul of marriage. I spent so much time preparing for my labor, taking twelve weeks of natural birthing classes in a hot, non-air-conditioned studio in the summer so I could be a master birther, but I didn't take any time gleaning the wisdom from experienced mothers. Oh, what I could have learned! How better prepared I would have been!

Another problem is that we focus so much time on babies but less time on understanding the very difficult season of toddler rearing. My most desperate days were when I was surrounded by a one-, three-, and four-year-old! While there are many fond memories of those years, the fact is they were hard! But they were a season, and with each season comes change, a new set of challenges, and many blessings. Now with my three-, five-, and six-year-old, I'm getting more sleep and enjoying the fact that they are more self-sufficient. They have amazing personalities, and we are friends. I love this stage. Each age has new challenges, but I'm learning the ways of motherhood as I go, and I'm also gaining tremendous perspective and even wisdom.

Remembering These Hard Times

I am choosing to remember the moments of desperation and the feelings of inadequacy. In fact, I'm glad I'm writing this book as a legacy to remind me of these days. I need to remember so when I'm older and have gained experience and wisdom, I can teach and train the younger women (Titus 2). I want to look back and say, "I remember how hard those days with little ones were. Can I bring you a meal or come over and clean for you or watch your babies so you can have some alone time?" or "Would you like me to show you how to____?" I want to be the one volunteering in the nursery; in fact, I want all of us who have raised our children to be the ones in the nursery, so that the moms of little ones don't have to be. Let's remember, so that we can be the Titus 2 women that our generation is so desperate for.

Sally

> *"In the twilight of our lives, we will be judged on how we have loved."*
>
> —ST. JOHN OF THE CROSS

Sheesh! Finally, after ten days, I have more than five minutes to myself! It is truly a myth to think that any woman can do it all. In my own life, I have found that if I am attending to the needs of my children, my husband, my busy home, my close friends, and my family, I really have to economize and prioritize my time. Life pretty much demands every moment! It can be such a constant challenge, but more and more with each passing day, I sense how important my role as a mother and godly woman is. I get such joy out of it as I daily see the results of my many years of striving toward the goal of being a woman after God's own heart and serving those around me for His glory.

Now, don't get me wrong, this certainly doesn't mean that I always have a pure, loving attitude toward these strange and complicated people who inhabit my home. But because of my love for the Lord, which is dearer to me each year, I keep putting one step in front of the other and see, with the eyes of my heart and mind, the power of my work to fill souls with great thoughts and love for God's kingdom. More than anything, I see more clearly how much I am a living picture of God's reality every day by exhibiting the fruit of the spirit, serving and giving of myself and my wisdom, and taking the initiative to speak joy and grace into the lives of those around me on a daily basis.

As you begin to revisit your ideals about motherhood anew, rather than give you a to-do list, I want to emphasize a few areas that might fuel the way you look at your own walk as a mother.

If you inhabit your role as a mother primarily from love, you will see God's hand moving in every part of your life. Love is the most important value to God. Jesus said the whole law could be summed up in two commandments—love God, and love people. He said people would know we were His followers by our love, and so it makes sense that our children will truly know we are His followers by the love that we show them. Love is the fuel that energizes every other type of growth. If you love well, you will influence your children, and your love will cover over many inadequacies.

As a consequence of that attitude of love, we must lay down our lives for our children, just as Jesus did for us: "Greater love has no one than this, that one lay down his life for his friends" (John 15:13).

The ability to last in motherhood requires giving up expectations for our own lives, deciding that sacrificing our desires and wants for the sake of our family is our gift of worship to our heavenly Father. To truly follow the example of Jesus, we have to submit everything we are to the faithful hand of God. Jesus gave up everything for His children, so that they would be redeemed. And so He became the model of servant leadership and sacrificial love. When we die to ourselves and our expectations, a lot of the desperate feelings leave because we are no longer seeking to fulfill our own needs and expectations as the ultimate good in our lives.

I don't, however, want to affirm a sense of punishment.

Following the example of Jesus in submitting our own will to God's doesn't mean we are called to live miserable lives where we punish ourselves through denial of anything good. I have a friend who exhibited such an attitude. She often talked about her constant prayer efforts and spiritual disciplines in a way that suggested she felt she was earning her favor with God by resisting every iota of her own will. I am convinced that at her core she was striving to figure out how to really know and serve God sincerely. Yet, because her heart attitude was about earning favor through denial of anything good in her own life, she saw God as a hard master who wanted nothing but work from her and was judging her when she failed. Consequently, it left most of the people in her life feeling guilty themselves, and they became somewhat cold and distant from her. She obviously understood the concept of sacrifice but seemed to have never found a rootedness for that concept in God's love and grace. She could only give out of a soul of performance, which, rather than blessing those around her, distanced her from them. She often spoke in religious phrases, and with each passing month seemed more cold and drained of life. So much effort, so little result.

As I pondered her life, I realized that when I am in the presence of someone who really walks with God, there is evidence of life, joy, goodness, well-being, grace, and faith. When one is washed with the unconditional love, grace, and mercy of God, the result is peace and thankfulness of heart. The few people who really exhibit the life of the Lord certainly aren't above discouragement or humanity, but there is a palpable sense of peace in their walk with God, having made a decision to trust Him through the ups and downs of life. My godly friends provide a sense of security for me, because I know their sails have been set toward the King and His kingdom. I can trust that their integrity will lead them in the right direction, because Jesus is at the helm.

I feel a rest in my relationship with them, because I know I am safe in the hands of mature, seasoned lovers of God who will love and accept me and point me to Him gently as we walk this road of life in fellowship.

One Saturday, we were getting ready for about a dozen people to join us for Easter lunch. Joy, age twelve, had peeled hard-boiled eggs to make an Easter family favorite, deviled eggs. Suddenly she was struck with a bright idea of how to make it easier, even though I had instructed her clearly and firmly on what she needed to do. The result of her idea was a mess everywhere—I have never seen so much egg yellow on the hands of any single person in my entire life! How in the world had she managed to make such a mess? One more thing at the end of a long afternoon of cooking and counseling another teen in our family. I'm certain she could sense my exasperation.

Suddenly, in that moment of irritation, the Lord gave me eyes to see this hormonal young woman as my sweet little girl, in the tumultuous throes of growing up. I could see the hurt and frustration in her eyes as she watched me clean up her mess. After I finished, I sat her down and told her how much I appreciated all the ways she had been available to help me with the several hours of work we had all done. I told her that I didn't always get my cooking right and how frustrated I often felt when I had put a lot of time into something like making bread or trying a new recipe, and it failed or tasted terrible. I told her I loved her and said, "I am sorry if I offended you in any way. You are such a treasure to me, and I know you were trying to do a good job. Thanks so much for all the ways you have helped me this week."

A few minutes later she climbed into my lap, all long, gangly legs and arms, and said, "I am so thankful that you always love me, Mommy." A kiss on the cheek and she was gone.

The older I get and the more I see my own selfishness and

immaturity, the more grateful I am that I know I don't have to perform for the Lord. He is mindful that I am but dust, and yet He still calls me His own special child. The amount of times in which He has been patient with me, loved me, and given me grace has made me so much more apt to love, forgive, and bear with my children, husband, and friends. I know they will make mistakes and be selfish and sinful just like I will. Yet I know that I can only please God and have peace in my own heart when I choose to love them back. In loving them, my own heart swells with more love and generosity.

Sometimes I will have a critical thought toward Clay or the kids. I know that if I foster the thought, it nurtures resentment. But when I choose to look at the relationship with eyes of love, to take the thought or attitude captive, I can get perspective. This is a person who is dear to me; I have a history with this person, and they have a personality that comes with many flaws, just as mine does. I need to remember that love covers a multitude of sin. Sometimes this means seeing the core issue at hand—an immature toddler or exhausted baby; a hormonal young woman or hormonal middle-aged woman; a somewhat distracted teen; or a worn-out husband from days of work.

I remember how much I need grace in all of my own fragile times. I also call to mind that I will please my precious, patient Lord Jesus if I obediently act in love. So I cover the person with grace, say words of patience and kindness, and then I am amazed that my feelings of love usually follow, and the relationship gets even better. This is not a formula that always works—I am not looking to always get the right results, as that is an unrealistic expectation—but it is a way of life that, because it has been practiced over many years, now turns my heart more toward loving, resting, and accepting others. In return, I find I am overwhelmed with the blessing of love that the Lord pours out into my heart.

I have learned that if I sow love, I will reap love, and it will be a blessing to me in return. All of this I have learned by placing myself at the feet of the One who emulated this heart of service even to His own death, Jesus.

Your Turn

2 CORINTHIANS 5:17: "Therefore if anyone is in Christ, he is a new creature; the old things passed away; behold, new things have come."

- Do you truly realize, in the deepest corner of your heart, that the failures and pain that have limited you as a mother have passed away through the love and work of Christ in your life? What are the new things that have come with your understanding of God's grace?

- How will this change the way you mother and love your children?

ISAIAH 43:18–19: "Do not call to mind the former things, or ponder things of the past. Behold, I will do something new, now it will spring forth; will you not be aware of it? I will even make a roadway in the wilderness, rivers in the desert."

- God is always about new creation. What "former things" do you need to forget?

- What "something new" do you want to see God do in your life?

- What is He doing already?

Something to Do

List out the dark and hard things of your past that you are struggling to overcome and forget. Be specific. Then pray over these things. Ask God's forgiveness where it's needed and His gracious forgetfulness where you are struggling to move forward. Then destroy that list. When that is done, make a new list of the new things you want to come. Dream. Ponder. Let God's Spirit fill you with excitement.

For a video on chapter 10, scan this QR code with your smart phone or visit http://bit.ly/VB3b1P.

Dear Sally,

Sometimes I'm not sure what is right for my life as a mother, or if there is a "right" answer. I get so lost with all the voices in my head telling what I should or shouldn't be doing as a mom. I want to push out the voices and just listen to God's voice, but sometimes I just can't discern. I also realize I struggle with people-pleasing. "What if so and so thinks I'm sinning?" How did you learn to push out people-pleasing and discern the One true voice?

Love, SM

Dear Sarah,

Voices of culture and expectations of others will always lead you to a feeling of inadequacy or a need to perform. Either they give you permission to compromise ideals or cause you great stress by not being able to accomplish unreasonable and impractical ideals. Recognize that God has never required more of you than you can possibly accomplish. So if you feel overwhelmed, it can often be because you are living by someone else's expectations. Be sure to follow women who are wise, whose lives have integrity, and whose advice rings true to your heart. Sometimes listening to women my own age and stage of life proved to be too much, as they did not have the wise perspective of living long and living well. I went against much of the advice that was popular in my time, and followed, by faith, what I thought I was supposed to do as I read God's Word. It has made all the difference. His ways and His voice will bless you as you learn to delight in Him, as promised in Psalm 1.

Blessings today!
Sally

CHAPTER 11

All the Voices That Influence Us

Sarah Mae

I have voices in my head, many of them actually. Some of the voices might speak truth, others may not, but the point is, if I'm not grounded in what I believe and why, then I will easily be tossed by the waves of opinion. I will be unsure, confused, and half-hearted.

I will also be overwhelmed and depressed.

The Voices That Mess with Us

There are different types of voices that mess with us. There are the whispers of lies that pump us with garbage and offer us nothing but poison. These voices sound like this:

- "Don't compliment your child too much or they will be vain."
- "You need to make sure you are doing X, Y, and Z in your homeschool."
- "Make sure you require first-time obedience."
- "You shouldn't be making any money."
- "You shouldn't let your kids watch that movie."
- "You should be good at cleaning by now."
- "You should always be submissive to your husband without any argument."
- "You're a bad mother if you give your kids french fries."
- "Your child should be reading by now."
- "You're not good enough."
- "You are a bad mother."
- "Why keep trying? You're just going to fail anyway."
- "Someone else should have had your children; they'd be better than you."

These are the hissings of the age-old garden snake trying to distract you from the truth. The problem is, they don't come from a snake; they come from those we trust, love, and see as authorities, and these venomous lies wound deep and can dig daggers into your spirit.

Then there are the voices of expectation. Here are some of my voices of expectation:

I expect that I can choose my personality. I think that I can morph into whatever personality is suited to what I think my children need at a particular juncture. I scour mom blogs for tips and encouragement on how to be a good mom, a good homeschool teacher, a good playmate, a good disciplinarian, etc. I find moms who are especially talented in a certain area and I think, *I can do that. I should be doing that.* I try those things, and then

I find that either I don't like them at all, or I'm just not good at them.

One area where I really struggle is in my children's education. I think many of you can relate. I homeschool, but this applies to whatever schooling you choose. There are tons of information/philosophies/curriculum for homeschoolers. You can go mad just thinking about it. Well, I came upon a wonderful blog where I read about a mom whose child was reading by four and a half years old, and I thought, *My child is five and not reading. I need to get on this!* I began pushing my daughter to read. I was afraid that if she couldn't read, it would show that I was a bad mother. I would get frustrated with my daughter when she got distracted (she's five!) or bored or tired or confused or had a hard time with words. Reading was not a pleasant experience for her or me. All of this due to my own insecurities of what people would think, and the false expectation that I should do what other moms do.

Thank God I have people in my life now who help me see that children are all different and learn at different stages. Mamas are also different in how they teach, and that's okay. I thought I had to be a certain kind of woman to homeschool, but that was completely false! I just had to want to do it and be willing to discover what worked for my family.

Here's another expectation: I think that I can do everything I set out to do. But I am an idea person. I am excellent at start-ups, and terrible at follow-through. Yet somehow I seem to think I can do it all, while telling people I can't do it all. Dichotomy? Why yes, that's me. I'm great at telling people that they shouldn't try to do it all, but I'm terrible at taking my own advice.

I thrive on ideas and putting them into action, but I sometimes forget to count the cost. Luke 14:28 says, "For which one of you, when he wants to build a tower, does not first sit down and calculate the cost to see if he has enough to complete it?" Oh, that's me, right here, not counting the cost. I just start collecting bricks and getting people excited for the tower to come. I am learning just how important it is to count the cost and not expect that things will go as planned just because I'm excited about them.

Recently Sally unknowingly showed me the principles of counting the cost when I asked her to do a project with me on the spur of the moment. I knew I had a great idea, and many people would join in, but Sally brought wisdom to the table. She said, "Your idea is really good, but I need to make sure I can do it well and follow through, and I'm not sure I can do that right now." In that moment I realized how often I jump into projects without fully considering whether or not I can do the project with integrity and follow it through to completion.

The truth is, I cannot expect to do everything I set out to do. I not only need to consider my options carefully, counting the cost and asking myself if I can honestly do the thing well and follow through, but I need to take into account the season of my life. I have little ones in my care. This is my time to invest in their souls, and to count the cost of not investing in them.

One more example of my unhealthy expectations: I expect that my husband should "get" me. Oh this. How many of us just wish our husbands "got" us? We want them to understand us in profound ways, and then accept us with open arms. We want them to admire who we are, how we're made, and who we are becoming. We want to be known and loved.

What happens when they don't "get" us? What happens when they don't understand why we have to leave the dishwasher open all the time, or why we like Taylor Swift, or why we can't enjoy our time away if our feelings are hurt before we leave?

The "I expect" voice is a killer of joy and true contentment.

My husband is not going to understand all of the inner

workings of my soul. He's not always going to think I'm fabulous, and he is not always going to agree with me (he might even think I'm crazy sometimes). Anyone who has been married for any significant amount of time understands these things and hopefully accepts them. When we let our husbands off the hook and are content to be who we are for the glory of God and not the approval of man, life is greener and more full. I want to please my husband, and I want his unconditional love, but he's a sinner just like I am, and humans can't really give unconditional love; it's hard enough just to love.

We've got to snuff out that voice or it will burn our marriages. Find contentment in the overwhelming fact that you are perfect to God; He gets you because He made you. Live free in that truth.

The One Voice That Matters

You all know this, but I'm going to say it anyway: there is only one voice that matters, and that is God's.

There are forty different ways to parent, but we need to ask, "Lord, how do you want me to raise my kids?"

There is only one person we are going to be accountable to at the end of our lives, and that's God. We are not accountable to all the people giving us advice or telling us what to do. We must listen to God. Go to the scriptures, ask for revelation, and listen. I had a mentor in college who used to tell me that God answers in three ways: yes, no, or wait.

We need to listen to His voice even when others think we're wrong.

We need to listen to His voice even when it's easier to take someone else's opinion.

We even need to listen to His voice when He points to how He made us.

We need to listen to our gut sometimes (maybe that is the Holy Spirit).

If I want to compliment my kiddos day and night and tell them they are good and important and beautiful, then I'm going to do that. If I know that God is doing something in my life even when others don't understand, I'm going to say, "Okay, God, I trust you with this so I'm going to dance it out as you lead."

It is so freeing to hone in on my Father's voice and push out the others. If you have many voices telling you how to act, what to do (or not do), or who you should be, might I encourage you to ask God to teach you to hear His voice? Listen to Him. He will guide gently. Approach His throne of grace, and push back all others.

If you know Him, you have His Spirit. Listen. "My sheep hear my voice, and I know them, and they follow Me" (John 10:27).

Sally

> *"What then is Apollos? And what is Paul? Servants through whom you believed, even as the Lord gave opportunity to each one. I planted, Apollos watered, but God was causing the growth."*
>
> 1 Corinthians 3:5–6

There is a certain danger of being a young, passionate Christian woman who has little confidence in being an adequate mother. The danger is a willingness to follow anyone who has a passionate and strong voice without knowing how to think biblically or wisely. There are so many voices in contemporary culture that it could make any parent feel overwhelmed.

Since the beginning of time, people have been listening to all the wrong voices. God was walking in the garden in the afternoon one day at the very beginning of creation, looking for His beloved children, Adam and Eve, to commune with them. But they had already been listening to the serpent, the wrong voice. God created them to be His companions and to follow Him. He offered them His guidance, love, protection, and wisdom. They instead chose to ignore God's voice and follow another. Following the wrong voice brought about sin itself—the compulsion to listen to any voice other than God's.

There has always been a dependence in humans on the opinions of others. We want exact formulas and rules, directions that will tell us step by step what to do. Yet from the moment of our fall as humans, when God began His plan to redeem the world, He has desired a people who will live in the tension and mystery of listening to Him, waiting upon Him, and trusting Him by faith.

It is no different today, in our modern world. God wants us to seek to be still and to know His voice. It is He who formed us, designed marriage as a beautiful paradigm for our benefit, crafted our bodies to be able to have children, and intentionally constructed the physiology of a baby's dependence on a mother who would nurse him and provide for his needs. Motherhood is God's creative and original idea, and He desires us to take joy in His intricate handiwork. He longs for us to seek Him, to rest in His love, to flourish in His acceptance of us, and to understand His ways for us with our children. When we follow the voice of God and rest in His ability to sustain us as mothers, we will find a true and lasting peace.

Motherhood is a topic in our culture today that elicits countless voices of opinion, polarized formulas, and arbitrary laws set forth by human imperfection. The voices in a mother's life can be overwhelming and destructive if not curbed by the true voice of the Holy Spirit. With the proliferation of media, the many voices of culture have found an even more catalytic method of spreading out and pushing their way into the minds of mothers who, if not protected by their own dedication to their walks with God through the guidance of Scripture, can easily be pushed to crisis mode in trying to sort it all out.

The rise of feminism has also robbed mothers of a sense of meaning and value. Modern culture—including many churches—often greatly undervalues the holiness of this calling and can undermine this role that God created to be important and of eternal value to the history and moral character of each generation.

I have found that trying to follow the voices of culture almost always leads to peer pressure, and unbridled peer pressure leads to peer dependence. Inevitably, those who succumb to it all too easily to give up for lack of guidance and support, being tossed to and fro in the sea of others' opinions for our lives. We will never be able to live up to someone else's expectations, but we are always acceptable to God when we live by faith and dependence on His grace.

Following voices without rooting them first in the voice of God can lead to legalism, which starves the soul of grace freely given by God. Legalism is rampant amongst Christian circles today, and many children have turned away from God because of harsh and arbitrary standards set forth by people who feign to speak authoritatively, but who either have no grounding in Scripture, or abuse interpretation of it for their own agenda.

Mankind has always wanted to make more rules out of God's wisdom than God ever intended. Jesus hated legalism and said of the Pharisees—the religious leaders who created and upheld the law and condemned others for not keeping every jot and tittle—that "they tie up heavy burdens and lay them on men's shoulders." He also called them snakes, vipers, and vehemently disavowed them in public (Matthew 23).

Many voices in motherhood today want to make a law out of everything—the activities that are best for a child; how to spank or not to spank, and how to secure obedience; working outside the home or staying at home; what clothing is acceptable for our girls; what movies, music, or books are or are not acceptable; dating or courting; adopting; drinking; even eating—there is no place where the grasp of legalism cannot and will not reach.

And yet, Scripture clearly speaks to the opposite. It tells us in Romans 14:22, "Happy is he who does not condemn himself in what he approves." The worry of what others are doing or are expecting us to do will indeed kill our souls. Even worse, it separates us from God's voice, the only voice that truly matters.

> You have been severed from Christ, you who are seeking to be justified by law; you have fallen from grace. For we through the Spirit, by faith, are waiting for the hope of righteousness. For in Christ Jesus neither circumcision nor uncircumcision means anything, but faith working through love. (Galatians 5:4–6)

Paul is very clear in Galatians that if we seek to be justified by the law, or rules and formulas, we have fallen away from the grace of God. Works never can or should equal God's grace. If we are trying to please people and follow all the voices in our lives, we will inevitably fall short. If we seek the approval of people regarding how well we measure up to their expectations or formulas in mothering, we will always fall short. If we look to a formula to provide all of the answers, we most certainly will fail. We cannot possibly please God with man's rules, because God doesn't share authority in our lives. He wants us to seek Him and Him alone, to live in the freedom and grace He has given us in figuring out our own life puzzles.

Follow the Voice of Jesus

There is only one voice to obey, and His voice brings life, joy, and freedom. God, as the designer, knows exactly how to guide us in our parenting. He is the only one who can help us pull off our lives with grace and freedom from guilt.

I could truly write a whole book about this topic alone. However, I will hone it down to the most vital concepts I have learned along the way.

Study God's Word and Ponder Jesus' Behavior

As I would seek in my heart to understand how Jesus lived His own life, and how He loved and reached the hearts of His disciples, it almost always led me away from the advice of others in my life. As I sought Jesus, I was constantly making decisions that did not fit into the box, and yet ultimately created peace, love, life, beauty, and joy in our home.

I am so very glad that Jesus did not create one box that He wanted all mothers to be stuffed into. Each family has its own puzzle, and there is abundant grace and joy in figuring it out through the example of our loving Savior.

Jesus was the servant King. He gave up His rights to live with His men. He taught them patiently, fed them, healed their family members, modeled to them how to live, and ultimately gave up His life for them.

He said of Himself that He was humble, gentle, and meek. He never sought to be prominent or important, or to please or impress people. Instead, He washed feet, touched those who had contagious diseases, and embraced and validated children when the disciples wanted to send them away. He lived a simple life, set firmly in the authority of His Father's voice.

Freedom to Be Yourself

God did not make cookie-cutter parents or children. Thank goodness He did not try to stuff all of us into one box. You have your personality for a reason—probably for the special work He has for you to do in this world. We have great freedom to live within the confines of our own personalities. The more we learn to accept our own limitations, and the limitations and vulnerabilities of our children, the more able we will be to give to our children from our strengths, rather than our weaknesses. Our happiness spills over into our parenting and creates children who feel loved and accepted.

Every family member is different. Some children are quiet, some are loud and active, some are artistic, and some love mathematics or are budding scientists. Some mothers are very nurturing, and some are driven to academics. Some fathers love outdoors and sports, and some are professorial types who love reading and writing. I am a very talkative, personable individual; God made me to be a speaker, and I love being able to understand that part of my life. Trying to cram any individual or family into the box of another is an insult to the God who made us all to be unique and different. He desires that we trust Him in the variations of each individual masterpiece He has designed.

Live and Love by Faith

There are countless verses that shaped my own parenting philosophy, and I have attempted to mold my own life around Scripture. As God revealed more and more wisdom during my time in His Word, and I practiced obeying these principles, I began to see my children respond to my parenting. As I began to model my role as a parent after the ways Jesus mentored His own disciples, I began to reach the hearts of my children with His truth and love.

Such an approach to parenting required me to live by faith and trust that God would show me how to love, discipline, and train each child according to their own design and their individual inclinations. I could also see that if I believed that God's Holy Spirit was with me and guiding me, I could surrender each day into His hands. Living that way took the pressure off me to find that obscure, only-right way to live. God is enough for my family and for my children. I have learned to live in love and obedience to Him and trust that He will lead me into a life filled with joy, growth, love, and freedom.

Your Turn

Proverbs 29:25: "The fear of man brings a snare, but he who trusts in the Lord will be exalted."

- Do you fear the opinions of people in your life?
- Why do you think that the fear of man brings a snare?
- What is more important: living the life God has set out for you, or living in a way that is acceptable to others?

Romans 12:2: "And do not be conformed to this world, but be transformed by the renewing of your mind, so that you may prove what the will of God is, that which is good and acceptable and perfect."

- What does it mean to be conformed to this world?

- Are there any ways in which you are conforming to this world?
- Can you be transformed if you are still relying on the voices of others?
- What does it mean to be transformed?

Something to Do

One of the most important things in life is to listen to God and not the world around you. Sit down, pray, and then write down what you know is true about God and what is true about what God believes about you. Decide what steps you will take in your life to ensure that you are living by God's voice and not man's.

For a video on chapter 11, scan this QR code with your smart phone or visit http://bit.ly/Tx6FB8.

Dear Sally,

I do not want to regret my life. I wake up at night in fear that in fifteen years I'll look back over my years with my children and think, I didn't do enough; why didn't I play with them more? *This is good for me because it keeps me on my toes. Sally, I want to live an intentional life, for myself and my children. I want to be a participant in my own life! I've let the last two years go, and I think,* Who ran my life? *How did you choose to live on purpose? What are some things you did?*

Love, SM

Hi, Sarah,

I am a purpose-driven sort of person. I have found that if someone can tell me why I should do something and it captivates my imagination, then I can stick to a task. If you understand that building your children's minds to become great thinkers and be filled with great ideas; teaching them to love well; inspiring them to greatness; giving them a legacy of celebrating life and loving God; and launching them into life as healthy, strong human beings is the best work for eternity that you will ever do, then you will have a reason to stay faithful. Define your purposes. Build your plan. Keep ideals alive, and it will fuel your reason to keep pouring excellence into this journey of motherhood.

Love, Sally

CHAPTER 12

Living on Purpose

Sarah Mae

I am a good-intentions person. I have plans and ideas, and I make lists, and I dream about all the ways that I'm going to change and be a good wife and mama and homemaker and writer. I am filled with good intentions . . . intentions I fully mean to integrate into my life.

I spend hours poring over homeschooling materials. I listen to inspirational audio about homemaking. I read books that encourage me to be a kind and loving wife. I desire to live well. But, as we all know, good intentions don't lead to a life well-lived; a life well-lived is accomplished when we walk each day in faith, keeping our eyes on Jesus and our hearts inclined to His Word.

It is accomplished when we choose right in the little things: to get off the computer when our little one wants us to read them a book. To cuddle when our children watch a movie. To kiss our husbands instead of push them away, so we can finish cooking dinner. To spend an hour making our bookshelf look ordered and pretty. To light a candle at dinner. To take the time to feast on the Word. To pray earnestly and with vulnerability. To hold our tongue when we want to scream. To hug tighter when we want to hurt.

Living out our intentions is not easy, but it is rewarding.

And we do have a choice. We can choose to live little by little, by faith.

Choosing to Overcome

Right now, I'm not depressed. In fact, I've gone for almost four months with no depression and no depressed feelings. Four months doesn't sound like a long time perhaps; for me though, it is. Last year I spent more days feeling overwhelmed, under-motivated, and depressed than I spent feeling alive. More bad days than good days. For a year. So when I say I've gone for four months without being depressed, it's a huge accomplishment. Now, I don't have the answer for everyone regarding depression (of course), but I can tell you a few things that have helped me to overcome.

I spent a year letting life happen to me. To the outside world, my life probably looked great. I got two book deals, my conference was a success, my blog was growing, I was able to travel and spend time with my sister and then my mentor, Sally, and I was being asked to speak at various events. All of these wonderful things were happening, but I was feeling lost and confused and really out of place. I didn't ask to be a published writer or a speaker or to have a platform. I was just a woman writing about life. And while I was grateful for all that was happening, I didn't enjoy it. I was depressed. I didn't want to do anything anymore. It was too overwhelming, and I didn't know what God wanted from my life. It felt like I was going against everything I believed in, doing all these extra things outside of my family. I felt like a fraud, a failure. I felt like a little girl who just wanted my daddy to tell me exactly what to do, so I didn't have to wrestle with all the decisions coming my way. I begged God for guidance, and He answered in an unexpected way (He does that, doesn't He?).

I expected that God would have me quit everything—blogging, writing, the conference—and just focus on my family and home. I believe strongly that my number one domain and priority is my family and the home sphere that I cultivate. That hasn't changed. But what God taught me was what it meant to walk in faith . . . and to make decisions in faith. Do you know how hard that is?! Faith.

Below is an e-mail my husband sent to me when I was trying to figure out what I was supposed to be doing with my conference, to quit or continue. I am sharing it here with his permission.

> I've been thinking about all the things that have been going on over the last week or so and it all culminating this past weekend with the conference. What is your calling (do you have one?). Here it is (I feel that it is from God): You, Sarah Mae, are first a follower of the Lord Jesus. Second, you are my wonderful, beautiful, and talented wife whom no other could ever measure up to. Third, you are the mother of three wonderful children. Fourth, God has given to you gifts and abilities/tools with which to greatly influence and impact mothers from around the nation to persevere as mothers, wives, and fellow followers in Jesus. He has given this to you with two separate book deals, a thriving blog(s), the first-of-its-kind blogging conference in the country with which

> to shout the name of Jesus and encourage women from all around to pursue the life that God wants for women and to do it with zeal. This is your calling. I believe as long as we ask God to provide us with the means to help take care of the first three priorities and don't say yes to anything that would sacrifice the first three priorities in order for number four to be done, then I believe continuing the conference and writing is the right thing to do.

Oh, how my husband freed me!

My very practical life is to bring up my children, day in and day out, teaching them, training them, and loving them through the moments. I need to care for my home, be hospitable, and cultivate wisdom, kindness, discretion, and purity. The big faith part comes in believing that I can use my gifts and strengths to encourage women outside my home. I have finally understood my calling, and that is to be first a wife and mother, develop a life of integrity, and then teach what is good via the platforms God has allowed me to have (books, blogging, conferences). I can also use my skill sets to earn an income for my family, as long as earning money doesn't interfere with my first priorities. I feel a sense of freedom now, and with that comes life. This is one of the reasons I'm not depressed anymore.

The other reason? Resolve. I've resolved to be in the Word every day. I've resolved to think about the end-game and what kind of legacy I want to leave. I've resolved to not let my thoughts get the better of me. I've resolved to overcome and not fade out. I want to persevere. I want to look back one day and say that I lived an intentional life, and I had integrity. I engaged in what life brought me, and didn't just let it happen to me. I was thoughtful and kept my eyes on Jesus, not pleasing man. I was a faithful servant. Faithful, trusting in Jesus' work in my life and not my own efforts. Any resolve that is met with results can be fully attributed to His work in my spirit.

Sally

> *"For which one of you, when he wants to build a tower, does not first sit down and calculate the cost to see if he has enough to complete it?"*
>
> Luke 14:28

When our family first considered moving to our beloved mountain home against the foothills of the Colorado Rockies, we began with nothing but an open and bulldozed plot of ground. What would ultimately become a place of refuge and comfort began with an intentional process of subduing all elements of creating a house and home. We were able to choose the direction the house faced, so as to find the best views of the majestic mountains around us. We were able to choose bright and vibrant colors for the walls: a rich, dark blue for Sarah's haven of a room, a gentle pink for Joy, and a kelly green for the boys' den. In the summer after we moved in, we spent a fun and muddy day sodding our front yard with lush, green grass. We put in a playground for the kids, a veritable fortress of imagination. Each wall in our home received pictures and paintings, memories from our journey as a family together.

In Genesis 1:28, God blessed Adam and Eve and then gave the command, "Be fruitful and multiply, and fill the earth, and subdue it; and rule." This concept of subduing an area doesn't just mean to rule over it in such a way as to tame it, but the actual context of the word means to exert your influence over something in such a way that is becomes subject to your leadership and becomes productive and fruitful. And so, this process of subduing our land, the design of our home, is a biblical term.

In short, we met every phase of developing our home with a subduer's eye, seeking to bring life, light, and beauty into our family's place of refuge. The process took us many months to complete and involved some difficult hours of labor along the way. We had to plan and focus on the details, and faithfully follow each step to its full requirement. When we finished, the reward was great—a world of comfort, joy, laughter, and life, for all of us to share.

Anything of worth takes effort and specific planning to bring it to fruition. As with a real home made of wood, siding, and roofing, the nurturing and development of our children is a process, in which each step presents unique challenges. I often found myself asking the same question over and over again: what am I doing to subdue or craft my home so as to bring to life the souls of my children? In the same way as we are responsible for the nurturing of our children's souls, so are we responsible for the nurturing and care of our own souls. What am I doing every day to ensure that I am walking forward with intentionality into filling my own soul with virtues of God's design for my life?

Before our children can reap the rewards of our investment in their souls, we must first nourish our own hearts and cling to the ideals God has given us as personal convictions. From our hearts flow the springs of life that God has begun in His goodness. Those waters will become a stream from which our children will find nourishment of understanding and growth for their own souls. Throughout all of Scripture, God, as a loving parent, provides us with the attributes with which to live full and soul-enriched lives, and seeks to help us graft those attributes into our daily lives, so that we may then pass them on to our children. Some of those qualities are:

Graciousness: what are you doing every day to engender gentleness and kindness to those around you? The things with which you fill your soul are the things that will shape the way you react to those around you.

Faithfulness: are you consistently responding every day to the callings of God upon your life? The way in which you follow through with the stewardships God has given you will be a strong example to your children of how to persevere in their own lives.

Godliness: do you seek God personally, with your whole heart, soul, mind, and strength, and do you practice it by reading and treasuring God's Word?

Each of these things, and many more beyond—gentleness, initiating toward other people, practicing love in the lives of those around you—will define the kind of person you will become. The more you invest in each of these virtues in your own personal life, the more you will be able to give back to your children from the wealth of experience you have amassed.

As you grow closer to God in love, faithfulness, diligence, and other such day-to-day practices, you will be able to more fully shape those values in your children's lives. A critical element to passing on those fruits from our own lives is to create a home environment in which those characteristics find firm footing. For Clay and me, we established our home with a foundation of love. It is God's faithful and ever-present love, made real and meaningful in our lives every day, which imbues in us a love for our children and a desire to see them grow in goodness and righteousness. That love was established by God through His Scripture, the cornerstone upon which all other elements of our lives were built.

From that foundation of God's love, worked out in Scripture, we built the metaphorical walls of our home environment around several strong pillars of practical, everyday practices. In a desire to see our children become strong communicators and thinkers, we provided countless books of strong literary and character-building value for them to read privately, and also enjoyed vibrant read-aloud sessions with the whole family. We also encouraged them to become clear and independent thinkers by having them write on a variety of subjects, and encouraged constant discussion of challenging ideas throughout the day, especially around the dinner table.

With the intention of creating habits of personal stewardship, we established consistent and reliable structures of responsibility. Each child would be given a list of chores and duties, expected to be completed throughout the day. This provided both a sense of expectation and accomplishment when tasks were finished, as well as a normative schedule that our children could rely on to be consistent throughout the week. We also encouraged our children to take stewardship for their environment and surrounding world, and sought out ways for them to invest in their local community. These activities included everything from community service to nature walks and visits to zoos and botanical gardens, instilling both a love for God's creation and a responsibility to care for it.

In a hope to see God's life made real to each of our children, we encouraged daily personal quiet times and provided biblically based tools for study of Scripture. We included family devotionals and Scripture readings in our daily schedule, usually at breakfast. This allowed our children to see Scripture as the source from which all other elements of the day sprang forth. We also involved them in a local church and encouraged them to invest their own gifts in our church community.

As an overarching premise, the more intentional we were with our lives, and the lives of our children, the more we accomplished in the long run. A lack of planning will inevitably result in a disappointing outcome. One particularly helpful tool I have often used as a way to stay consistent to each of those practices is to write out all my goals in my journal. I have found that rather than trying to bring to mind intentions from memory—and feeling guilty when I am unable to do so—having my goals in written form provides a tangible thing to turn back to when I feel unmotivated or disorganized. It also allows me to prioritize the most important things in my life, and put what is less vital on the back burner. The more you have practical touchstones in your life to which you can turn, the easier it will be to walk forward into an intentional path for both you and your children.

As you seek to find footing on this path toward intentional motherhood, developing a plan to bring forth your ideals into each of your family members' lives must begin with your own walk. Just as when creating a real home—laying a strong foundation and raising up walls, bringing color and landscaping, providing a sense of comfort and belonging—so will your intentional actions and personal practice create a strong structure of God's grace and purpose in your own life and in the lives of your children. It takes a personal embrace of God's call to subdue, to bring life, and to practice a consistency of conviction.

Our family's mountain home provided us years of comfort and joy and an environment to experience the vibrant fullness of life. In the same way, if we accept this call to subdue our souls and our children's souls, we will eventually reap the reward of our intentionality invested for eternal purposes.

Your Turn

Proverbs 14:1: "The wise woman builds her house, but the foolish tears it down with her own hands."

- Who is responsible for building your children's legacy?

- What do you need in order to build a house?

- What does it mean to be a foolish woman or a foolish mother?

Proverbs 31:27–29: "She looks well to the ways of her household, and does not eat the bread of idleness. Her children rise up and bless her; her husband also, and he praises her, saying: 'Many daughters have done nobly, but you excel them all.'"

- What will be the results of your hard work and efforts if you follow God's design for you in building your children into a godly legacy?

1 Corinthians 10:31: "Whether, then, you eat or drink or whatever you do, do all to the glory of God."

- Ultimately, when we meet Jesus face-to-face, He will say, "What did you do to whisper the secrets of the kingdom of heaven into the hearts of your children? How did you glorify me in your home?" How will you answer those questions?

- Who is the real person we are supposed to please in the labor of mothering?

Something to Do

In your journal, list five ways you want to leave a legacy to your children. (For example: loving relationships, moral excellence, a vibrant faith, etc.) Under each area write at least two practical goals or ways you will implement your plan this year. Make a six-month plan for specific ways you will establish routines or traditions to build these goals into your schedule.

For a video on chapter 12, scan this QR code with your smart phone or visit http://bit.ly/PoSVHl.

Dear Sally,

You inspire me so much when it comes to living a full, beautiful, adventurous life! I want what you have created for yourself and your family. I know all families are different, but can you share with me some ways you crafted a beautiful life?

Love, SM

Sweet Friend,

Enjoy yourself. Cook food that you love. Play music that inspires you. Buy flowers and candles because they please your heart. Celebrate life in your home in the ways that bring you pleasure. Cultivating the art of life in your home not only brings you happiness, but it makes your home a lively, fun, fulfilling place. Most of all, enjoy life and celebrate it every day. God created pleasure just for us, so live in that blessing.

Off to my own pleasure today! Remember—lighten up and enjoy!

Sally

CHAPTER 13

The Art of Life

Sarah Mae

The conference I hosted had just ended, and I finally made it home; but I was not alone. My blogging friend Logan missed her flight, and I had invited her to spend some time with me, so I could get to know her better. One of the things I learned on the way home was that she was an interior decorator. She has a knack for color and coordination. I don't. Decorating and I are like distant lands. I'm Greenland; decorating is Iceland. And my home reflects my serious lack of decorating ability. You can imagine how giddy I was to have an interior decorator sitting in my living room with me who was willing to offer her skill for my plain home. So we did the most fun thing we could think of.

We went on a shopping spree to Target.

I told her the colors I'm drawn to and some of the styles I like. She immediately grasped my eclectic spirit and launched into decorator zone. She grabbed curtains and pillows and a zebra-printed ottoman (which I almost stopped her from getting, but she convinced me I'd love it). We went home, and with barely enough time to spare before we had to leave to catch her second flight, she transformed my living room from a lifeless, dull space into a beautiful haven of beauty and warmth. And I loved that zebra-striped ottoman.

She made me feel so special, taking the time to use her talent to bless me and my family. She created beauty around us, and to this day every time I sit in my living room, I sigh a happy sigh. She did for me what I want to do for my children. I want to offer them a space where there is life and beauty and warmth. I want to spend time creating beautiful places for them, giving them something to see and touch and look forward to being in.

I want them to feel loved by how I cultivate their surroundings.

We will all feel more alive when we tend to our domains, when we choose to give life to the areas we inhabit. We don't need a Target shopping spree to accomplish this; we just need to be willing to take the time to craft life.

I think we'll all feel a little more alive that way.

Sally has been teaching me so much about what it means to invite beauty and adventure and art into my family's life. It is the little touches of love and intention that can spur a soul toward feeling alive. Children don't want a dull existence. They thrive on adventure! I want to provide a sense of fully living to my children. I want to enjoy them, and them to enjoy me, and for us to enjoy life together.

Recently it was my birthday, and I wanted to go out for breakfast. I called up a few people, but no one could come along. I looked at my babes and I said, "Who wants to go out for breakfast?" Of course they all did, and so we got in our van and took off for the quaint little restaurant we go to from time to time. This was my first time taking out all three children by myself. I was always afraid I wouldn't be able to handle them alone. (I have mentioned I have a bit of a wild-spirited child, right?) But we went, and I told them to get whatever they wanted, and we enjoyed a birthday breakfast together. We feasted and laughed. We got away from the house, the mundane of the everyday, and splurged on life together.

It's the little things, remember?

If you have taken the time to model what it looks like to make someone feel special, your child just might exhibit that same love toward you. Not too long ago I was asked to do a Scripture reading at church. As I mentioned earlier, our family worships together, so our little ones sit with us in the sanctuary on Sunday mornings. I went up to the podium, read the Scripture with umph, because that's just how I am, and when I was finished, I heard clapping—a lone clapper. I looked around and saw my four-year-old son standing up with smile, clapping, and saying, "That was awesome, Mom. You did great. That was awesome!" You know my mama heart just about burst, right? I was so overwhelmed with his carefree attitude, unable to contain his pride for me. He didn't care that he was the only one clapping or standing; he just was so proud of his mama that he was compelled to act. My precious, passionate son taught me to be unabashedly willing to stand up and say, "Great job. You are awesome!" And I want to be that person for my children. I want to be their greatest fan, cheering them on, affirming them, and beaming with pride in the Lord for them.

The Duties That Kill the Joy

I think sometimes we mamas forget, or lose sight of, or just don't know how to enjoy our children because we get so caught up in our duties as mothers. We worry about their schooling and their diets and their playtime and their bedtimes and their chores and their salvation and . . . You get it. We worry. We want the best. We want to be good mothers. We fear messing up, or coming up short, or just plain failing. At least I do. I can get so bogged down in all I have to do that planning beauty and adventure is just another thing that takes work and will exhaust me. And that might be true, but it's better than drowning in the mundane. It's better to put some energy into getting into life than letting life just happen.

But the real trick to joy, I'm finding, is to focus on the good things. The fact that we even worry if we're good mothers or not is a wonderful indication that we probably are. We care enough to worry! We want to do good by our children. We want to raise them well.

And isn't it freeing to know that you're going to mess up? I mean, you're certainly not going to get it all right! We will fail. We will have regrets.

We will have grace.

Sally

"Lord, I crawled across the barrenness to you with my empty cup uncertain in asking any small drop of refreshment. If only I had known you better I'd have come running with a bucket."

—NANCY SPIEGELBERG

"This is the day which the LORD has made; let us rejoice and be glad in it."

PSALM 118:24

Being awakened in the middle of the night at three thirty, I began to sink into a panic that I wouldn't be able to fall back asleep. My mind began to dart every which way to all the stresses in my life. Finishing writing a book, going on the road for a family wedding after what seemed like a painfully short respite at home, finishing the college scholarship and loan applications for one of my children, and countless other things were weighing on my mind.

Eventually, having resigned myself to the reality of sleeplessness, I got up and made myself a cup of tea. Sitting in the dark, I could suddenly sense the Lord whispering into my ear, "Don't neglect to see the beauty of the life around you while being overwhelmed by the duties of life."

I turned on my Pandora music channel, lit small vanilla candles placed strategically throughout my living room, and asked God to open my eyes. I began to thank God for the sweet children He had placed in my life. Desiring to be close in spirit to Sarah, my eldest daughter, who is, even now, across the sea in Oxford, England, I went to the computer and read her blog.

There I found a newly posted essay about the life-filling, energy-producing, always beautiful and confounding joy of God. Though far from her geographically, the thought of her had led me to her precious words on her blog, and I immediately felt closer to her. It made me able to go forward into my morning with a little more courage.

Only a couple of hours later, Joy, my second daughter and youngest child, came bounding down the stairs wearing her favorite owl pajamas. I looked up at her and began to marvel at this wonderful sweet one. What a darling bundle of delight God had allowed me to enjoy in my home today. How glad I was to not be alone, but instead to have the opportunity to look happily in her big brown eyes, to sing at the top of our lungs together, and to listen to all the fun and mysterious secrets on her heart. Being present to celebrate such a special moment filled my heart with joy.

Joel, my six-foot-five-inch-tall son, my music man who just finished studying for his degree in music composition, soon appeared in the kitchen, where he began to wash dishes, humming as he placed the tea kettle on for a cuppa. How grateful I was that this intelligent and highly talented dish-washer had been home for a brief three months in the interim of his life to be my friend, to accompany me on trips, and to share in mutual thoughts, ideals, and dreams. It almost seemed as if God was speaking to my heart, "He won't be around much more—look at him and take in the moment."

Finally, my energetic golden retriever, Kelsey, came bounding over to my chair the moment I sat down with a plate of scrambled cheese eggs. *You are always so accepting of this old mama*, I thought, *a picture of unconditional love from God's hand every day to me.* And so I got up from my comfy chair, left my breakfast, and made her a scrambled egg—much to the guffaws and pleasure of my kids.

God lives in my home, but sometimes I ignore Him and don't hear the music He is playing just for me. This journey of mothering is a challenging marathon of moments, hours, days, months, years, and decades. And yet, in each moment, God has sprinkled across our paths beauty, love, and joy. We have only to cultivate eyes in our hearts to observe this Artist's work of life. Whether it be a baby patting his mama's chest as he gurgles milk, or a toddler giggling and screaming in fear at the sight of a frog; a little girl pretending to be a princess all dressed up in pink, or a little boy who spilled the milk one more time and longs for the gentle voice of grace from his mom; even a hormonal, reactionary teenager growing up and straining toward adult life; all of these moments and passages have the mystery and grace of God in them, just waiting to be unpackaged as evidence of His love.

Our shoulders often falter under a constant weight of performance and duty. We get caught up in the hectic cycle of endless tasks and often end up finding our lives to be a barren wasteland of burdens. We ask half-heartedly for a sip of His grace, never fully expecting Him to listen and answer. Yet Jesus wants us to come for a bottomless lake of His mercy, joy, fun, love, forgiveness, power, beauty, adventure, and freedom. He desires to give us eyes to see every moment from His perspective, looking out with a view over all of eternity—and seeing the stark difference between what really matters and what will soon pass.

Over the years, God has taught me to celebrate the infinite possibilities of what each day might hold. Choosing to look for the very fingerprints of God in every part of my world, as evidence of His love, has become a central life goal. However, living a life of joy and contentment and imitating Him in our homes requires a willingness to see our lives through the lens of God's eternal perspective. He is wild, way beyond our control, and more interesting than we can imagine with our limited minds; but far too often we live in the mundane and don't see the miracle of the moment because the eyes of our hearts have become blind to His reality.

C. S. Lewis understood the truth of it:

> If we consider the unblushing promises of reward and the staggering nature of the rewards promised in the Gospels, it would seem that our Lord finds our desire not too strong, but too weak. We are half-hearted creatures, fooling about with drink and sex and ambition when infinite joy is offered us. We are like ignorant children who want to continue making mud pies in a slum because we cannot imagine what is meant by the offer of a vacation at the sea. We are far too easily pleased.

To me, one of the beautiful graces of a strong woman is the ability to see the true value of her own life and the lives of her children, and to celebrate them every day, as Jesus did. It was Jesus Himself who gave the example of treasuring children; He took time out of His busy day to hold them, to tousle their hair, to bless them.

Choose to Be Thankful and Practice Being Content

To move from feelings of desperation to delight requires that the eyes of your heart and the attitude that you express be ones that exemplify God's own heart and attitudes. We must come to accept and agree with scripture that "children are a gift of the LORD," and that "the fruit of the womb is a reward" (Psalm 127:3). We must fit our heart to agree with God's heart.

If every morning you look at your child as a gift from God, a blessing that He has bestowed today, and thank Him for that blessing, you will approach your children with love, patience, and grace. You have to bow your knee and say, "God, you really are good and you knew exactly what you were doing when you gave me this child." Your heart will not *feel* contentment and joy until it is aligned with the voice of God's Holy Spirit within you. You will develop strength and fortitude in the attitudes you choose to practice and exercise. If you develop muscles of praise and thanksgiving, you will come to find increasing strength and stamina in those very practices.

As a result, true joy, coming from God's Spirit, will bubble up in your soul. You will begin to see that your children are developing their own attitudes of gratefulness. Those around you will be blessed by being with you. A dedication to strengthening yourself in God's Spirit will reap an exponential reward in both your life and the lives of those around you.

Put Away Distractions That Steal Your Joy

Television, cell phones, Facebook, blogs, social networks, and media of every kind are prevalent and prolific in our lives. We are so accustomed to such things that we hardly even know anymore how to enjoy the natural and "unplugged" moments in our lives, spending time in nature or treasuring experiences with loved ones. The modern person no longer walks into such interactions with a peaceful sense of contentment in the moment, but rather a frenetic restlessness, constantly wondering if, while gone from technology for a few moments, someone has left a comment, e-mail, tweet, or Facebook message—all distant and impersonal interactions.

The truth is that Jesus made us to be intimate with our family and friends. Only in personal and close interaction can relationships satisfy the deep longings that all of us have to be known and deeply loved. If we cannot find a way to substitute an addictive, virtual faux-reality for the opportunity to build intimacy and shared joy in the lives of our children, we will never pass on to them the concept that God is loving, present, intimate, and responsive. I often see women who have become so used to a substandard life that they cannot see that they have become empty, shallow, and impatient with the real live human beings right in their midst, who are longing for love but are also so ready to give back generously.

Make a Commitment in Your Heart

Experiencing the deep fulfillment of being cherished is one of the best rewards of my life. Investing in love has paid off with dividends far beyond what I could have initially imagined in my relationship with my children. They are my delight and best friends.

Yet this process developed by faith, and over an extended period of time. I had to behave as though I loved and cherished my children even when the feelings were weak or hidden. Learning to be patient and really listen to them when I was exhausted was a commitment I had made long before finding myself in such situations. I had resolved beforehand to focus on saying words of life and encouragement when I really wanted time alone; to use a gentle and respectful tone when I was tempted to express anger. It was out of the belief that these commitments mattered to God that I made them. The core of this concept is that feelings will follow obedience. The more I practiced love, joy, peace, patience, and all the other fruits of the Spirit, the more I found myself loving such attributes in the depths of my heart. It was as though God gave me these children, so that I could grow up and become all that He had designed me to be.

Children see through the lack of integrity of a mom as they grow older. If a mom is not living out her words of love by giving love, her children will learn to not to believe her words. It is so vitally important that we live with integrity by choosing to worship God in front of our children through all the moments of our days. Celebrating God and all His attributes as well as His blessings creates a winsome energy that fuels a child's own desire to follow hard after God. When a mom practices seeing the miracles and joy of God's own making in all the moments of her day, a child will hunger after the same heart attitude.

Your Turn

Proverbs 24:3–4: "By wisdom a house is built, and by understanding it is established; And by knowledge the rooms are filled with all precious and pleasant riches."

- Bringing beauty and traditions to our homes provides us with the opportunity to craft a home that is pleasurable, comfortable, and inspirational. How can you fill your home with treasures of life that build faith, love, close ties, and a sense of family history?

- What kind of atmosphere do you hope your home will reflect?

Psalm 19:1: "The heavens are telling the glory of God; and their expanse is declaring the work of His hands."

- As we view the stars and the sunsets, we see a part of God's artistry and the beauty of His work. How can you manifest the work of your hands by the creativity and art you personally reflect in your home?

Something to Do

In your journal, write down three ways that you would like to craft traditions, meals, and design in your home that will make it a more life-giving environment. Plan the materials, the work, and the ways you will implement this in the next month.

For a video on chapter 13, scan this QR code with your smart phone or visit http://bit.ly/QEuQJp.

Dear Sally,

I finally feel like I'm beginning to overcome my feelings of inadequacy. I'm accepting my limitations and trusting God with my life and my children's lives. I owe so much to your kindness and wisdom over my life. You have blessed me deeply, and I will forever be changed by your investment in my spirit. Thank you! I'm going to keep persevering; I will be a participant in my own life. Now, let's start making plans for a European getaway!

Love, SM

My Friend,

I always wanted to be a hero—to sacrifice my life in a big way at one time—and yet, God has required my sacrifice to be thousands of days, over many years, with one more kiss, one more story, one more meal. After putting one foot in front of the other for so many years, following His ideals of home and family, now it has become my greatest joy. My heart followed what my ideals led me to embrace. I adore my children and they are my best friends. We celebrate life together and always want to talk to each other when we have news or fun or sadness to share. Our family culture is so defined and the deepest blessing of my life. I couldn't have known how much satisfaction it would bring me to have crafted this life from my own soul through God's leading.

You have a brave, loving, generous heart, and I am so very proud of your willingness to hold fast and to pursue these ideals. You will find the roots you always longed for, the memories you shaped as treasures, and children who will generously honor you because you were willing to invest. I have seen you grow into such loveliness and conviction. Hold fast, put away unnecessary guilt, and pursue ideals, and you will find the blessings He always wanted you to have.

I will always be here for you.

Your forever friend, Sally

CHAPTER 14

Desperate . . . Not Defeated

Sarah Mae

I was in the church nursery on nursery duty when a foster dad brought in a sweet little crying baby girl with pierced ears and dark curly hair. He had just picked her up the night before, and he and his wife were fostering this little one until her parents could get her back. My heart went out to her immediately as I held her. She wouldn't stop crying, but she was so precious and tiny, and I felt only love for her. Holding her prompted the longing in my heart to adopt.

My husband and I have been waiting to adopt until our wildfire sweetness Caroline was a little more . . . containable. But now she's three and I think within the year we'll be ready to open our arms to another child. We just had to get out of the "desperate" season first.

When I originally thought of the idea for this book, I was in a place of desperation, and I saw so many other women who were right there beside me. The thing we all have in common is little ones. With some perspective, I can see that having little ones is a season. For some, that season is longer than others, but children, Lord willing, do grow up. And they do get easier in many ways. My oldest is only six, so I can't speak to any age past that, but I can say that I don't feel desperate anymore. I have my "curl up in the closet and cry" days, but overall, I'm good. I'm almost out of the season of very littles, and I'll be moving into a new season with all the ups and downs that it holds. Also, if we bring a new baby into our home via adoption, the season will be different, because I won't be caring for more than one baby at a time (unless God has a sense of humor). The point is, no matter how desperate we feel in certain phases of our lives, we are not defeated. We may feel absolutely bone-weary, and hormonal, and depressed or a little nutty, but we'll get through it. We will.

You will.

I acknowledge that you might be someone who needs very practical help right now because you think you might lose your mind. And you might, for a while. But you have a faithful God who loves you and whom I believe will bring you what you need to get through. There is no one answer for everyone, because the Lord works differently in each of our lives, but you need to know that He hasn't forgotten you. He doesn't forget His children, big or little.

If you do go through this season of desperation alone and without help—though I pray that does not happen—then I want you to write down what you're experiencing and how it affects you. Put in writing how you are going to be there for your children one day and the other young women God puts in your path and be the helper you never had.

I want you to think of all the times you have said . . .

"I wish I just had someone to help me with _______."

"Why don't any of the older women ever volunteer in the nursery?"

"I've been praying for a mentor, but so far, no one has shown up."

"It seems like all the older women don't want to invest in the younger women. Where are they?"

"I just need a break . . . I need to breathe."

"I have no money, so I can't go anywhere when I need to get away. I could just really use a night away alone."

"I'm drowning in laundry! I wish I had some help."

You have probably thought many of those things, and more. You recognize that you need help, you need time, and you need refreshment. I want you to commit right now that, Lord willing, you will be that person for a few young women one day. I want you to tuck into your heart that one day you will help a young mother with her laundry. That one day you will open up your home for a young mother to come and spend the night to have some quiet time alone. That one day you will volunteer to be in the nursery, so a young mother doesn't have to. That you will make yourself available to mentor and teach young women. That you will be the help you desperately wish you had right now.

Will you commit with me to be that woman one day, Lord willing?

I will too.

And you know what? You will be good at it, because you will have compassion. You will remember what it was like to feel alone and desperate, and you will be happy to give your time and whatever energy you have left.

You know what else we can do? We can raise our children to help others. We can teach them and show them how to care for young mothers in the church. We can show our daughters how to serve the body by encouraging them and training them to go to the homes of young mothers and be their helpers . . . without charge. Our daughters can cook meals for young mothers, babysit, and clean in order to serve them. We can be the change-makers. You and me, friend, we can be the change.

There is a lot of talk out there about dreaming big dreams and going for them. We're told we should "follow our callings" and "pursue our dreams."

The thing is, during the season of life when you have little ones, it's important to be sensitive to our time and limitations.

The God who gave you your gifts and talents is the same God who gave you souls to bring up, train, invest in, and disciple. I don't know what His "dream" is for you, but I know that Scripture is filled with admonitions for a mama to make her home her focus and bring up her children. A mama's primary domain is her home. This doesn't mean you don't have another purpose that God wants you to fulfill while you're breathing on this earth, but your first and main purpose is to deeply invest in the souls He's given you, and you will struggle immensely if you do not have resolve regarding your role as a mother.

I want you to know that I have struggled with my place in this season of life. I want to be faithful and have integrity with my family and give myself over to them, but I'm not immune to feeling the "call" of other opportunities that distract me from my main role. Sally has taught me that a wise woman manages her time; she doesn't necessarily give up everything, although sometimes she must.

Since I have chosen to continue writing and hosting a conference, I have had to learn what it really means to walk by faith.

I also have my husband who is a great support, and he encourages me when I get off balance. He also offers me opportunities to work on my writing and the conference, and we have a sweet woman come over for a few hours once a week to clean our home and play with the babes. I am also limiting my travel. My husband and I agreed that I would not become a speaker who travels many times a year until and unless we can take our whole family. Right now we have decided that I will travel to speak around three times a year, and that's it. I'm telling you this because I want you to know that I am a deeply convicted mama who believes wholeheartedly that there is nothing more important or sacred than being an intentional mother whose time is focused in the home. I am also a deeply committed follower of Christ, and if He leads me in faith to write and teach, I will, again, within boundaries and not in place of my primary role. I consider it a heavy responsibility to bear. If I'm going to spend any time away from my family, it had better be worth it.

My ultimate encouragement to you so that you don't feel defeated? Give in to your season of life. You will feel desperate sometimes, I know, and it's scary some days. But the more you allow yourself to be fully and completely invested in the discipling of your children, the less defeated you will feel. And don't forget to do what we talked about in an earlier chapter—carve out time for yourself. Everyone needs to have life-giving activities or time away, or they'll eventually burn out.

Sally

> *"And hope does not disappoint, because the love of God has been poured out within our hearts through the Holy Spirit who was given to us."*
>
> Romans 5:5

Sixteen-year-old Joy, my youngest child, was sitting in our breakfast nook one morning recently, adorned in penguin pajamas, munching on toast and scrambled cheese eggs, and hosting a face deep in contemplation. "What is swirling around in that mind of yours?" I asked.

"Mama, it has all finally sunk in. You have been building habits of working hard, foundations of moral character, a love for reading and writing, manners, and priming our hearts with messages of faith, God's love, the story we will tell—and I don't know why, but all of a sudden the whole picture of life is clear to me. I'm just so thankful for you being such an amazing example in my life."

It was a defining moment for me. I had now finished most of the foundations and shaping of my children's souls, and all four had come to a point of owning their lives. By God's miraculous grace, they all love us, have a strong heart for God, and are passionate and alive with dreams for their own lives. It is truly a grace.

However, I came to realize over the years that the forming of their souls was a hard, long-distance race. In retrospect I can now see how it has become an essential part of my spiritual service of worship to God. He entrusted these precious souls into my hands. The work of motherhood was the way He wanted me to serve and love Him. I have always found my source for this inspiration in the way Jesus was willing to lay aside His life to serve and love His disciples and those around Him, and to invest in their lives. In order to stay the course, we mothers must see the nurturing of our children as a spiritual call in order to have integrity in our own Christian lives. If parents, especially moms, don't take up the banner of responsibility for their children, to protect and teach them what they need to believe and understand, who else will? Our children must grow into the adults who will carry the stewardship of the gospel into their own generation.

It can seem overwhelming, for certain. That is why, as mothers, we have to begin by cultivating our own souls. It is a truth I wish I had known earlier in my own walk, that a wise woman first takes responsibility for the well-being of her own life. Just as you train your children and bring life and growth into their lives, so God desires to do the same in yours. So often as mothers we are so overtaken with busyness and stress that we lose focus and drift from that center place of trust in God.

The core of allowing ourselves to be shaped and nurtured by God must begin and end with a heart attitude. Scripture tells us that what a man sows, he will reap, and that as a man thinks, so is he. My question to you then is, are you choosing in your life to cling to God's goodness and instruction in righteousness? Is your heart turned toward Him in a posture of trust and submission, as an earthly child to your heavenly parent? Is your own soul being formed by His Word and the power of the Holy Spirit? The call to train up a child is more than a one-time choice; it is a day-to-day, long-term commitment to shape your children, the greatest gift that God has given you stewardship over. The attitudes and choices you practice now in your day-to-day walk will determine your ability to endure the distance in your ideals. These heart attitudes are not complicated or difficult to understand, but rather moment-by-moment choices made throughout the day. As Scripture says, if we are faithful in these small things, God will entrust us with much, knowing we will be up to the challenge.

Your soul is a garden, ready to bloom with beauty if tended carefully and faithfully through the many different seasons of life. Consider the challenges you face every day as an opportunity to till the soil, and trust that when you do, God will plant the seed that will bloom into grace and goodness. God desires to fill our lives with an overflow of His blessing, but only soft and well-tended ground will produce the fruit of God's master Gardener hand. So practice cultivating those heart attitudes in your life. When you are tempted to turn to negativity and dissatisfaction, see it instead as an opportunity to develop a heart of contentment and trust in God's faithfulness. When you are caught up in the mundane of the everyday, seek to turn your heart toward joy, and celebrate the goodness that God brings into all parts of life. When you are tempted to despair or give up on your ideals, choose to engage your heart in God's grace, which extends far beyond your own reach. When you are exasperated by your children, seek to love them and see the potential in them, knowing that in whomever God begins a work, He will be faithful to complete it in His time. And remember that God loves you as a parent loves a child, and sees you as a work in progress as well. Turn your heart toward being faithful to the end, knowing that God will never leave or forsake you in your journey.

Making such choices alone can feel overwhelming. Thankfully, God made us, so that we would be drawn to rely on the help of others. Jesus Himself said that two are better than one, and that a cord of three strands is not easily broken. He calls us to bear each other's burdens, and to seek each other out. In your walk, actively look for other women, both of similar age to you, and those who are older and more mature, who can feed into your life. The support systems you build will uphold you when the weight of your struggles are bearing down upon you.

In garnering friends and advisors close to you, seek out those who hold similar values and convictions to your own, and who resonate with your ideals and convictions. It is far easier to walk through life with someone if he or she is headed in the same direction as you! In my own life, I have a dear friend, Phyllis, who has been a faithful comrade in arms through many seasons of my life. I intentionally seek her out, both as a kindred spirit and as someone who, when I am with her, causes me to want to love God even more because of her own faithful walk with her heavenly Father. When someone can laugh with you in your happiest moments, carry your sorrows with understanding, and affirm the choices of conviction you make without hesitation, you will stand a far greater chance of facing the many challenges that mothering brings.

Additionally, and equally as important, it is essential to make time in our lives regularly to find rest, to refill our own souls. It is impossible to give life and depth to our children if we have no reserve from which to draw. Throughout all of Scripture, God provides His Sabbath as a means of providing this rest. It is a gift He gives, knowing our need for taking a beat in the frenetic rhythm of our lives. Raising up godly children is a long-distance race. Long-distance runners pace themselves, knowing they will need to reserve energy for the whole length of the race. It is no different in our own lives as mothers.

God also calls us to rest, so that we will be able to listen to His voice. There are so many loud noises in our lives that draw us away from God's gentle whisper. When we quiet our souls before Him and close off those outside sounds, we can once again hear His words, and be led by Him in goodness and truth.

Ultimately, the hands that are growing the gardens of our souls are the hands that hold us close to our Father's heart, a Father who has promised never to leave or forsake us. Our hope is in the One who has been faithful throughout all the ages to those who have stood fast and clung to Him, knowing that He is faithful to complete the work He has begun in us. The soil of our gardens are made up of hope that does not disappoint, but rather brings to full bloom the beauty and grace of Jesus' character, our ever-faithful master Gardener.

Your Turn

Revelation 21:7: "He who overcomes will inherit these things, and I will be his God and he will be My son."

- Seven times in the book of Revelation, God says that he who overcomes will be blessed in some way. Throughout this book, we have spoken of the many ways we all encounter difficulty and challenge in our walks as moms. In what ways is the focus of your heart the most important part of overcoming the difficulties and becoming one who lives victoriously throughout all the days of motherhood?

2 Corinthians 12:9: "And He has said to me, 'My grace is sufficient for you, for my power is perfected in weakness.'"

Psalm 103:13: "As a father has compassion on his children, so the Lord has compassion on those who fear Him."

- As a loving father, God cherishes helping us with all of our burdens. With the God who created the whole universe on our side, what qualifies you to complete your journey of motherhood with grace and confidence?

- What is God's heart attitude toward you as a mom?

Something to Do

Spend time in prayer with God. Search your heart and see if there are any burdens you are carrying that He wants to carry for you. Confess any inadequacy you feel and accept the mercy, compassion, and help, by faith, of your heavenly Father. Now place your burdens in the file drawer of heaven and decide to leave these in God's hands.

For a video on chapter 14, scan this QR code with your smart phone or visit http://bit.ly/XQIVqk.

Conclusion: Living the Story of Motherhood for Eternal Legacy

"By wisdom a house is built, and by understanding it is established; and by knowledge the rooms are filled with all precious and pleasant riches."

PROVERBS 24:3–4

My sweet friend Sarah,

I have found as I look back on our friendship that I have grown to love you as though you are one of my daughters. I hope that some of what I have written here will help you and all of the other sweet moms who read this. As I have said before, living out the reality of being a godly mother and seeking to pass on a legacy of righteousness through my children has been more challenging and stress-laden that I could ever have imagined.

And yet, now that my children are all grown and my last one is entering college, I know without a doubt that investing in their lives intentionally and faithfully for so many years is the best work I will ever do before I see Jesus face-to-face. I have watched them develop into adults who have strong convictions and passionate love for God and His kingdom, who are close friends and companions to Clay and me, and who are great thinkers and communicators. All of them are growing more effective in their own arenas as they pursue their life's work.

Having been God's architect in shaping and building them into these kinds of people has been more deeply fulfilling than I ever could have imagined. In seeking to give them excellence in all of these areas, I found that they have shaped and built my soul, faith, mind, and heart.

A mother, living well in her God-ordained role, is of great beauty and inestimable value to the future of any generation. Her impact is irreplaceable and necessary to the spiritual formation of children who will be the adults of history to come. There are so many things that make up the world of a well-nurtured child. Fun, comfort, humor, graciousness, spiritual passion, compassion for the lost, hospitality, chores, meals, training, life-giving words, hours and hours of listening and playing, praying and reading and instructing in truth—all are parts of the mosaic that go into the process of soul development.

Because God wants us to better understand Him as a parent in our own lives, He created us to be stewards of our own children so that we could be involved in this great kingdom work of building real people into godly adults. His design was to engage us in His work, and through that work, He shapes us into His own image along the way. The process of cultivating our children into excellent, healthy, and strong adults requires someone willing to put in hours, days, weeks, months, and years of diligence and endurance.

I am so excited and proud of you that you are willing to devote yourself to this great calling. I wanted to leave you with several areas of encouragement that I hope will help you along the way.

Stay Strong and Hold Fast to Your Ideals

I have to admit that the course of motherhood is so much longer and so much harder than I ever thought it would be. Many days I was weary, confused, depressed, and fearful, and wanted to throw in the towel. Always remember that it is not sinful to be tempted—all of us are tempted to compromise our ideals, and all of us become weary in great tasks. Yet it is how you respond to these obstacles in the course of your life that will determine the telling of your life story.

One morning recently I was experiencing some very dark and overwhelming thoughts about some circumstances I was facing. Yet, because these sorts of thoughts are not a surprise to me, I knew that I could go to the Lord and give them to Him and simply wait for Him to show me how to move forward into these challenges by faith.

The story of Jacob came to mind. When Jacob was sleeping one night, an angel came to him and provoked a wrestling match that lasted through the night. Though Jacob could not overcome the angel, he held on tenaciously, clinging fast and refusing to yield. Finally, as morning dawned, the man who was wrestling with Jacob requested for Jacob to let him go. Jacob had such a devoted and diligent heart that he replied to the angel, "I will not let you go unless you bless me" (Genesis 32:26).

Jacob is a picture of what God wants us to do—to prevail, to keep holding on, to seek Him and expect Him to bless us.

Interestingly, another concept came to my mind as I was studying this Scripture. In the book of Revelation, the prophetic and epic final chapter in the history of Scripture that teaches about the end of the world and the coming of Jesus as King and Ruler over all, the word *overcome* is used seven times. This intrigued me. When God repeats anything over and over again, it is, more often than not, very crucial to something we are meant to clearly understand.

When I did a study of this word, I found it has several aspects to it. The first is to fight until one is victorious in a battle. Another meaning is very much like the concept laid out in Jacob's story, to prevail—to mount up over and endure until one conquers the battle at hand, by staying fast until victory is achieved. Hanging in there until the end—this is our story of integrity and faithfulness.

This, to me, is such a picture of what a mother is called to be: a warrior who will not give up or cease to keep fighting the battle for her children's souls. There are so many battlegrounds in which to fight and prevail—the work of a home, the discipline of children, the training of their character, thinking of ways to make your life and home interesting and fun, so that your children will have a safe haven in which to spend time, spending hours and hours as a counselor and friend to answer heart questions and to sympathize with hurt feelings, nurturing depth of thought about God, working through dreams and disappointments. All of these important roles take a great amount of time and energy. And not only once, but over and over again, consistently pushing against sin and embracing God's truth, until our bodies, souls, and minds are weary.

The overarching truth, however, is that you are building a legacy of people who will flourish in their lifetimes, hold fast to the gospel, and have an impact for the kingdom of God. Your labor is not in vain; it does defeat mighty strongholds and brings righteousness to bear. But you will have run your race well if you intend to reach the goal of your ideals; it will take a continual refreshing and renewing of them in your life.

Satan knows that the righteousness and faith of the next generation are in the hands of parents, and particularly the moms, who interact with their children every hour of the day. Satan would just love for us to think our labor is in vain and ineffective, and that we are not adequate for the task. And yet, in every case in Revelation, overcoming is always rewarded with a great blessing—a new and glorious name; to have your name written in the book of life; to have Jesus speak about you before the Father; and so much more.

As I have looked back over my own journey of motherhood, I see clearly that the cultural voices during my early years of motherhood always gave me permission to compromise my biblical ideals for my family. But God wants us to be those who prevail, who are willing to engage in the fight and to hold fast, waiting for His blessing.

Please keep this image in mind when you are tempted to feel discouraged. There will be many times in the battle when you feel you are at your end; the stakes are so great. God, if you seek Him with your whole heart and commit your ways to Him, will help you give to your children a story of a woman who inspired faith, and who built a legacy in her home of righteousness, grace, and truth. Your children will perceive you as the hero and champion of their lives if you hold fast.

I have found it so vital in my own walk to keep a journal and write down my commitments. It has enabled me to stay strong through all the seasons life brings. I imagine that I was planting a metaphorical flag of commitment, saying, "I will follow God's path for me and His call on my life as a mom, to be faithful as Jesus was for my whole life, no matter what. I am making this commitment to be a servant leader, as He is, so that my children will always have an advocate for their lives, as Jesus is my advocate."

Accept Your Failures and Limitations as a Part of the Process

Three children had pneumonia, chicken pox, and encephalitis in two months. I was so sleep-deprived that I wandered around my house in a stupor. Burst eardrums had accompanied the encephalitis, and my sweet ones had borne much pain. It was like a marathon of trials and temptations, and all of this followed a very difficult miscarriage. Never-ending dishes and medicine and blankets and baths in skin solution and dirty towels had taken its toll on me. The hazards of house warfare had created in my weary heart feelings of failure and insecurity. "If I were a good mother," the voices would whisper, "I would have been cleaning as I went; I would have read Bible stories to them; I would have made homemade meals, I would have . . ."

Without realizing it, I was allowing myself to have a pity party, and I was giving in to what I believed everyone else was thinking—Sally is not a very good mom. It happened slowly, this slow slide into insecurity, as though a little rain cloud had been mounting over my head and had now become a shower of accusations.

I was sitting on the couch thinking about the messes everywhere. Sarah appeared from behind the door and lay her head down on my lap, and as she did, she grabbed one of my hands and began to stroke it, looking happily up at me.

"Mama, you are the most beautiful woman I have ever known. I am so glad you are my mama. I just love the way your hands give me love and make me feel better when you rub my head and tickle my soft back (our family term for a back rub). I am so glad God gave you to me! Let's always be friends."

My heart suddenly filled with warmth and joy again. It was as though I realized in a flash that the work I was doing was heart-work. My success was not defined by the externals, but by investing time, love, comfort, and care into the lives and hearts of the little ones given to me. I could suddenly see the hours of dedication and love would be there in their brain and heart memories forever.

Failing so many times to live up to ideals was just part of my journey. I would yell, feel guilty, and then ask for forgiveness; get out of control of the house and then stop all activities and get it back together again. Selfish bouts of rage would occasionally take over as I longed for my own life as an adult, and I would sulk in depression. There were so many ways I failed in my own flesh. Even so, over time, I learned to like who I was and accept the fact that at times I would inevitably fail in my ideals. I learned to live in the reality of Romans 8:1–2: "There is therefore now no condemnation for those who are in Christ Jesus. For the law of the Spirit of life in Christ Jesus has set you free from the law of sin and death." It became a foundational truth for me.

Please, sweet friend, don't measure your worth to God by the times you fail any more than we would be upset with a toddler for acting in an immature way. I have realized that to the Lord I am a toddler and He knows my limitations. "He is mindful that we are but dust" (Psalm 103:14). He is not surprised with my little tantrums, but He is committed to helping me grow up in Him, to become stronger and more mature as I exercise my spiritual muscles.

Expect God to Work Powerfully and Engage Your Heart in Faith

Finally, the key element to seeing so much fruit in my own journey of motherhood was that I learned to take God at His word! It may seem like the most obvious concept in the world, but I have become convinced that faith is the key element of the power behind my commitment to be a good mom. Each day I say, "God, you have access to my children's hearts, souls, and minds. Please, through your Holy Spirit, make the life of Christ real to each of them. Lord, help them to have a desire to obey and to learn self-control. Please show me how to be the mom you created me to be."

Hebrews 11:6 says, "Without faith it is impossible to please Him, for he who comes to God must believe that He is and that He is a rewarder of those who seek Him."

There is, if we are willing to accept it, a heart-engaging attitude of dependence that God desires for our lives. "Lord, I want to be your girl and I want to please you with all that I am and all that I have. So I will daily throw myself into loving, training, teaching, and discipling these precious ones you have entrusted into my hands. I will offer you my fish and my loaves—all that I have I will give. I know that I am not enough, but you and I together are what my children need. Lord, fill in where I am inadequate. I know that you are the source of my wisdom, my strength, and my success."

There is something about this release, giving it into His hands, choosing to enjoy each day because of knowing He loves you no matter what you do, and seeking to cultivate joy that will bring an energy to your home that is far more than you could ever create on your own. God is so willing to bless us, but we have to choose to believe He is with us and that He is also at work behind the scenes. This kind of faith, trust, and engaging of your heart is the secret of seeing the life of Christ and the blessing of Christ grow in your home.

When I found myself confused, I would seek Him. When I was fearful, I would hold fast to His promises. When I needed perspective, I would read the life of Christ and ponder Him and the ways He influenced all those around Him.

Thousands of days of reading His Word, praying, and connecting my heart in faith to Him became the source of my spiritual growth. I began to see that the reason He gave me my children and the responsibility of their care is that it was a perfect way of conforming me to the image of Christ. As I needed Christ and His ways, I would copy Him and depend on Him, and my Christian life would become more authentic.

As I look back on this journey, without even realizing it at the time, I can see now that He deepened my love for my children, stretched my capacity to work, gave me a more excellent mind, and developed my own civility and graciousness as I sought to teach all such things to my children. In fact, by submitting to this great task, I can say, by His grace, I am so much more the person I would have wanted to be. In following the will of God, we always experience the love of God and the blessing of God.

Sweet one, this is your life, and you have the opportunity to live a story that your children and grandchildren will be speaking of for generations to come. They will say, "My mama/grandmother, Sarah, left us such a courageous life to follow, so much generous love, such passion for the kingdom of God and celebrations of His beauty and feasting in her home that people from everywhere wanted to love the God she loved because of the life that was in her."

You are exactly the mom your children need. He created you for these good works from before the foundation of the world, and as you walk this great call of motherhood with Him holding your hand, you will be amazed at how He weaves the beautiful thread of redemption through the pattern of your life. He brings light to the dark places through you, something you could only have accomplished by embracing His wonderful call and embracing these very precious children who were inextricably created as part of the design for your life. May He bless you and fill you with great joy in this journey.

Sending my love to each of you and your precious ones.

Sally

For a video on this Conclusion, scan this QR code with your smart phone or visit http://bit.ly/Xb0QZq.

Q & A with Sally Clarkson — Your Questions Answered

I receive thousands of questions every year about specific areas of motherhood and how to do it well. Below are some of the most common questions, and they are just a beginning. We will have more online to encourage you, inspire you, and give you some great ideas.

Before you read these answers, I would like to encourage each of you to find freedom and grace to live within the limitations of your own family puzzle in such a way that cooperates with your personality and with the gifts God has given you. There is no one "right way" or formula to follow for every family, mother, or child. Live in the freedom of faith and the abundant life Jesus came to provide. Understand that children are a gift, and God has hidden blessings and lessons to teach us as we seek to please Him in taking care of this gift He entrusted into our hands.

Most of all, seek to enjoy your children and love them and you will be happier, less desperate, and more fulfilled little by little. Motherhood is a long journey. I wanted to keep having more kids so I could do it right because I grew into the role and became wiser with each passing year. But in spite of all of my weaknesses and mistakes, God's grace filled in the cracks, and I have four healthy, vibrant, purpose-driven children who still love Clay and me and God!

Question: *How can I make time for me to "breathe" when I have a husband who works sixty hours a week and I am taking care of three little ones by myself about twenty hours a day? What are things I can do to make it through five to six days of being a "single mom" and remain a patient, graceful mother to my kids and a wife to my husband after I've been going, going, going without a break for days?*

This question applies to all moms—especially single moms, moms whose husbands travel, and moms who have no support systems!

No mom can find the grace and strength to hold fast to ideals in this journey unless she establishes a regular time with the Lord, who gives grace and help every day. Here are just a few ideals to keep you refreshed and encouraged.

- Spend time in the Word daily. Filling my mind with truth is the attitude adjustment I usually need, and when I find that my heart embraces the role of motherhood as my service of worship to Him who gave me my children and who destined me to be a mother, I tend to be more willing to love and serve my children!
- Remember God is the only one who can meet your needs. "And my God will supply all your needs according to His riches in glory in Christ Jesus" (Philippians 4:19).
- Begin and end your day with prayer. Pray for much-needed energy plus "love, joy, peace, patience, kindness, goodness, faithfulness, gentleness, self-control" (Galatians 5:22–23).

- Pray for your husband, the father of your children, so that he can be more open to filling this role as a dad. Dads need grace and patience as life is taxing for all of us and they are also often lonely and exhausted.
- Cultivate a heart of gratitude. The book of Proverbs reminds us, "Be careful what you think, because your thoughts run your life" (4:23 NCV). Thus, be grateful for your husband, his job, and all that it provides.
- Find an older, more mature Christian mentor to hold you accountable.

Question: Is it important to take "me" time and how do I fit that into an already overpacked schedule?

Each mother must make a plan for growing personally! Honor your personality and make a plan to fulfill some of your most prominent felt needs. A wise woman learns to manage her personal life! Here are some suggestions:

- Get extra rest. There are days that going to bed early is the best option over all other choices.
- Include time to work on special projects or personal interests (scrapbooks, painting, blogging, reading, gardening, etc.).
- Start a moms group to encourage others—and to build like-minded friendships. The more you give, the more you receive.
- Build a support system of friends who are willing to help you out (babysitting co-op, play groups, etc.).
- Phone a kindred-spirit friend. I find a meaningful conversation both stimulating and helpful.
- Keep things simple regarding housekeeping, cooking, and obligations.

- Find ways to keep your sanity (exercise, hire a sitter, social interaction, daily quite time).
- Ban yourself from nagging and complaining about your husband's travel, financial limitations, how hard your life is—or anything else. Do not practice comparing your life or limitations to others. What you water the most is what will grow, and the weeds of a whining spirit will choke your own joy. Remember that husbands need to feel appreciated.
- Also remember that your children long for a happy mom. If you expect them to be patient, content, and self-controlled in their own heart attitudes, you need to grow in this in front of them—they will model what they see.
- Plan a night out with friends or something special several days after a home routine is established. This gives you something to look forward to.
- Give yourself grace to grow and grace to make some mistakes.

Question: What are some hints for managing my time since my husband travels or works long hours?

Growing together when apart:

- Create a travel calendar especially when dad must be gone for an extended time. Include outings, obligations, and a welcome home celebration.
- Plan fun outings while dad is away. Do a local search for monthly family outings and events in your area. Choose a few to do (a library reading for kids, free museum days, etc.). This gives kids something to look forward to and keeps everyone occupied.
- Have dad map out where he will be so the family can follow his travels, a.k.a. a geography lesson.

- Have kiddos hide notes or pictures in dad's suitcase.
- Dad can leave behind a special token with kids.
- Moms should create an event the kids can look forward to (for example, sleeping once in a while with mom while dad is away).
- Establish a daily time for dad to connect with the kids. Have an ongoing game they play together (Scrabble, Draw Something, and others).
- Have kids share high and low points of the day with dad.

Growing closer when together:

- Welcome dad home. Warmly greet your husband with a hug and kiss and teach your kids to do the same.
- Create a cheerful atmosphere when he returns home. "The heart of her husband trusts in her, and he will have no lack of gain. She does him good and not evil all the days of her life" (Proverbs 31:11–12).
- Ask about his trip and meetings.
- Be sure to have a date night soon after he returns.
- Don't forget that men spell love and appreciation S.E.X.

Question: *I am desperate to break the negative patterns we have set and I have modeled in regard to communicating with one another, giving each other grace, and putting other's needs above our own. I hear how my boys talk to each other and I realize they are imitating me. I'm desperate to change and don't know where to begin. I'm doing so many things right, but I feel like I am sabotaging myself with my overreactions and overtraining.*

Our children are a gift to us in this area, aren't they? There's nothing like living day to day with children to show you exactly where your own soul still needs work!

You've hit the nail on the head here (and sorry it feels like your own)! Many times I too have been saddened by seeing my children treating each other unkindly or impatiently, only to realize I've acted similarly. So take a deep breath, mama. You're not alone. Best of all, the Lord is with you! And He is able to help you change.

No one is ever going to achieve perfection this side of heaven. That being said, we carry a great responsibility toward our children because we are the example they follow—sometimes subconsciously!

As moms, we need to take our sins—our selfishness, impatience, frustration, etc.—to God and ask Him to forgive us and change us. I try to focus on one area at a time and that gives me bite-size goals on where I need to mature. His Word promises that the fruit of the Spirit is love, joy, peace, patience, kindness, goodness, faithfulness, and self-control—and we need all of those as moms! Ask Him to fill you with His Spirit and to remind and stop you when you're headed down a wrong road in your attitudes. He is faithful. He will cover your mistakes and help you change! When you see motherhood as your service of worship to Him and that how you treat your children is your obedience to Him, it gives more importance to treating our children as He would.

Training is also a key here. Helping children grow from immaturity to being loving and graciousness and having self-control happens over years—not days. Clay wrote "Our 24 Family Ways," and we taught them to our children so that we would have an objective value to point them to when correcting them. For instance, number 5 says, "We treat others with kindness, gentleness, and respect." And we teach them the corresponding Bible verse.

When they violate this family way, we go back to what they have memorized and say, "Do you think you are treating your sister with these attributes? How should you have spoken to her differently?" Or "Hitting or yelling is not allowed in our home." This way, when you have trained them according to your biblical values, you can go back again and again with objective correction that they have learned and heard, and eventually this training shapes the values of their minds and hearts.

I thought my boys would never get along, as they are quite opposite and close in age. But now they are the best of friends and love to spend time together. Remember, training and maturity take time. They were each other's own training grounds, as all of our children are to each other.

Question: Will they be okay? In the end, after we train them up in the Lord, when we raise them in His word, after all is said and done, will they grow to love the Lord like we have raised them and want them to?

Oh, how I wish I could give you a simple answer to this question! Raising my children in the nurture and admonition of the Lord has been the joy and honestly biggest challenge of my life. It has required much prayer and dedication; swimming upstream against the cultural norms; many sleepless, fear-filled, and prayer-filled nights and work-filled days. But now, looking at four whole-hearted children who love the Lord and are affecting the world for Him, I know all my hard work was more than worth it!

That being said, I do have dear friends who lived in a similar manner with their children, who worked hard and prayed and loved well, and yet their children have chosen a very different road. I know their hearts break and there is continual prayer over these children who seem far away from the foundations their parents built so carefully.

So why bother? Why work so hard if there is no guarantee that our work will have the result we long for? There are many reasons that could be given, but I'll share the two most important in my heart.

First, embracing my role as a mom is a matter of obedience. The Word says, "Whatever your hand finds to do, do it with all your might" (Ecclesiastes 9:10). It also says that older women are to teach the younger to love their children. Jesus gave me the example of laying down His life for those who followed Him; of cooking for them, washing their feet, walking with them day by day, teaching them to pray, and so many other wonderful, beautiful illustrations of love. I want to obey Him.

Second, I want to live my life with no regrets. I want to spend every moment I can serving, training, encouraging, blessing, disciplining, and loving my children so I can look back and know I did everything possible to show them the love and glory of God. I can't guarantee they will choose Christ. But I can make sure I light a clear path and put as few roadblocks as possible in the way.

But rest in the Lord, love your children generously, train them not to be selfish, and celebrate life with them, and they will probably in this atmosphere of high love and high training respond to you and love the God you love. Be still and know that He is God and He will reward and bless you—it is His nature.

Question: *How can you still influence, teach, and talk to your kids once they are older teens—junior high age and beyond—or is it too late? It seemed much easier when they were younger.*

In my experience, taking my children out one-on-one is a great way to get at the real issues of their hearts. Also, I made time with them when they were willing to talk, such as at bedtime, about their day. Sometimes teens feel embarrassed to share all the battles and thoughts and temptations that are going on in their hearts. They need to feel that you will not react and condemn them for telling you how they really feel. Do not ask them questions of the heart in the "public" arena of the family. Give them the honor of being alone with you to share important things.

If you make time for them in a way that speaks their love language, they will more likely open up to you. I would take my boys out to breakfast by themselves, ride with them when they drove with their music throbbing and blaring, just to have that opportunity to speak into their lives. I would take my girls out for lunch or to shop for an afternoon. But it was their choice and their places of interest as I stayed in their worlds, and we are close to this day.

All teens are raging with hormones and have a healthy desire to be independent so that they can become mature and strong while still, at times, wishing for a "mommy" to meet their needs—a world of conflicting emotions. The more you understand their battles and desire to be loved by peers and give them a foundation of security in their relationship with you, the more they will hold fast to your values and your faith.

All of my teens went through a time they had to question life and what they had been taught in order to grow strong in their own convictions. But, mama, you hold fast, love generously, train them still when you are able, and believe in them with life-giving words. And making cookies and buying them coffee or having their friends over always helps too! Be the home that the kids like to come to—then you know where your children are and who they are with!

Question: I hate to admit it, but sometimes I don't even like my children and they drive me crazy.

I used to feel guilty about my negative feelings. Sometimes I didn't even feel like being a mother. Sometimes I didn't like who my children were, yet God told us to "love our neighbor as ourselves," to fulfill the law and prophets.

And so I realized over the years that my commitment to love them did not always mean I would have happy, loving feelings. Maybe you need a break. Sometimes a whole night of sleep without anyone "needing me or touching me" helped me feel better. Getting away and doing something fun—making some time for you—may lessen your resentment. All mothers feel these things if they are alive!

I have learned that loving my children, and my husband, was more about my choosing to love them and extend God's grace every moment I could decide to do that, and not an issue of how I felt. I am sure a soldier in war doesn't feel like getting shot at, but if he is courageous and faithful, he will carry out his duty of being brave and giving his life because it is the right thing to do. Whether we like it or not, our life (attitudes, actions, and words) directly influences and impacts our children's lives. Children learn through watching and imitating. Like sponges, they absorb our lifestyle as parents.

Question: My children seem so different. One is obedient and compliant, and my other little boy is so active and loud and it is hard to get him to obey me. How do I apply consistent discipline with such different children in my home and how do I maintain fairness?

Remember to study your children. One of the biggest mistakes parents often make with older children is to treat them all the same. However, they are each very unique. We should strive to be a student of each of our children. This takes time, but the payoffs are invaluable. Reaching our children's hearts, which is our goal, means looking inside of them and finding what they love, value, and listen to, and seeking to appeal to them on the basis of who God made them to be.

And remember, God gave boys testosterone so they could be warriors. Don't punish your little boy (or little girl) for acting out how God made them!

Don't try and make them like you or another sibling. Also don't play favorites as you can look at Scripture and see the effects of jealously among Joseph's brothers. "His brothers saw that their father loved him more than all his brothers; and so they hated him and could not speak to him on friendly terms" (Genesis 37:4).

Watch your children while they work or play and see where each child is gifted. Validate that area to them. As you identify weaknesses, help them get necessary help and work with them on these areas little by little. Don't micromanage or overcorrect your children as you will become a police figure and it will dishearten your child. As you witness their strengths, you can lovingly guide them in that direction.

Question: Will my children become too dependent on me if I allow them to cry and cling to me when they seem irrationally fearful or shy?

Knowing your children's fears allows you to come alongside them and be a source of comfort. When children are left alone with their fears, they begin to worry and grow anxious. Help them with your presence, comfort, and a listening ear, pray for them, and remind them that God is always close and cares for them. "Be anxious for nothing, but in everything by prayer and supplication with thanksgiving let your requests be known to God" (Philippians 4:6).

Also, if some of these areas persist through the years, you might look for symptoms like clinical OCD or autism or other issues. Get input, read, pray for insight, and be gentle with your little ones. Usually they will grow out of fears and insecurity, but be sure you are meeting the felt needs of your children enough before expecting them to "get over" something. Sometimes their clinging or grumpiness is a reflection of a mom's neglect, not the child's attitude.

Question: What do I do when my children have been injured by a circumstance or family member or by divorce? Will my children be victims?

Our children will experience many hurts during their lifetime such as death, divorce, shame, embarrassment, neglect, rejection by peers, failure, abuse, trauma, illness, etc. This is a time to offer a listening ear, tender touch, compassion, and comfort. If you are feeling inadequate, remember the source of your strength is Jesus, and that He will supply all you need. The Bible says, "Blessed be the God and Father of our Lord Jesus Christ, the Father of mercies and God of all comfort" (2 Corinthians 1:3).

We should not seek to keep our children from pain, as this is a fallen world, and they need to understand biblically how to stay fast in a world of difficulty and temptation. When they have trouble or are hurt, enter into their world of feelings, struggles, and questions, and then sympathize with their honest emotions.

Then always lead them to the hope and purposes of Christ. Tell them how God causes all things to work together for good. Explain to them that they will grow stronger through their pain and that God will develop compassion in their hearts for others in similar situations. Always help them know that failure does not ever have to define us. Failure and pain become foundations for wisdom and understanding and strength to face life's battles.

Really knowing your children's love language is also helpful. If it's time, give them yours. If it's words of encouragement, speak generously to them about how special and wonderful they are with their unique personality.

Ask yourself: What do my children love to do? What brings smiles to their faces? What do they talk about? What do they spend the most time and money on? Then join in and do those things together. Have fun while creating memories.

Question: When you have a highly active and strong-willed toddler (mine is three), how do you choose your battles? At what point (or in what situations) do you simply let it go and at what point do you put your foot down in authority and demand compliance? Help!!!

So many moms try to micromanage every single behavioral issue with their children and feel a need to win every battle, especially when they are young. As I observe how God treats me, I realize that I keep learning and growing in my weaknesses, sometimes in areas I was not even aware of. It seems He shows me one area at a time.

And yet, other parents let their children misbehave and be out of control so much of the time that their children are a burden to all who come into their wake.

And so discipline is an issue of training, little by little, year after year. Do not expect a toddler to behave like an older child who naturally has more self-control and maturity. Learning to be consistent in teaching and training is a way of life. It is quite exhausting if a parent makes everything an issue for the child and the parent. And be sure to enjoy each stage of your children—have fun, giggle, distract, lighten up, and win their hearts. Children are more likely to respond to discipline if they feel loved and affirmed. Be sure to extend grace to your young children, and also make sure they have lots of time to play outdoors to wear out their energy and fill their need for activity.

Question: What do you regret doing or not doing when your children were young?

I wish that I would have trusted God more and worried less. I regret not being more careful about the voices I listened to. Thinking back now, I should have enjoyed my kids instead of worrying whether I was always doing it right. I definitely wish I had spent more time just loving them and letting them know how much I loved them.

Question: As a working mom (and also the family bread winner) am I failing my children by not being home?

Choices have consequences. Our children will become most like the ones they spend time with and will take on the values of those who validate them the most. So if you work and leave them in the company of others most of the day, they will naturally love and be like those with whom you leave them.

There is no formula for every family. But building a godly generation in your home requires a plan as all great works do. You have to look at your own family puzzle and make a plan that is tailor-made for you. I knew that our ministry as a family would require a great deal of work from me so I often went to bed at 9 when the children did and worked from 4:30 or 5:00 a.m. until 7:30. I had to make sacrifices to my personal needs in order to be able to embrace my high ideals for my family.

Many moms make the mistake of not writing down or planning what results they hope for in their family. Planning helps you determine the choices you will make. Ask: How am I going to pass on my faith? What values do I want my children to have? How does my plan cooperate with my priorities for them? How can I manage my life in such a way to meet these ideals?

The verse that always went through my mind was, "What does it profit a man to gain the whole world, and forfeit his soul?" (or the souls of his children) (Mark 8:36). If you must work, pray for God to give you ways to invest in your children and to put them in the company of people who have your values. And remember, God is there to support you. I have seen many different kinds of families work well, when they have God at the center of their plan.

Question: *How do I encourage my son to be a boy without squashing his spirit? I desire so much to love, nurture, and encourage his spirit, but I feel that often I squelch it instead.*

Spend time alone with your son and ask him questions to help you know who God made him. Read hero tales to him, from the Bible and from life, to give him something great to imagine so that he will have great men to model his life after. Play Legos and board games with him. Let him spend time outside after reading him some exciting books that challenge him with new ideas. Give him a cape and a plastic sword, and teach him to be heroic and act out the battles he reads about. Let him work his testosterone out in appropriate places and every day. Allow him to play loudly and rigorously.

Teach and train him, and all your children, about outside play behavior and voices versus indoor, church, or company voices and behavior. Encourage him to be strong internally by choosing to exhibit self-control and then validate him for that. Train him before you get into a situation: "We are going to a concert and I want you to use all the inside strength you have. This is a place to show mom your strong self-control and sit still in your seat, don't talk during the concert, and then afterward we will celebrate and do something special."

Encourage your son to read biographies of inventors. Give him broken appliances or items in the house and let him take them apart and invent new items. Go on field trips with him, and when you come home, let him tell you what he learned and have him draw pictures. Also, don't limit boys to girl books and movies.

Question: How do you know when to give your children freedom to make their own choices (music, TV, books, friends)?

The most important thing to do is first establish your own family appetites. We had music at the dinner table each night and went to concerts together as well as movies. Set the standard for whatever is true, good, and righteous (Philippians 4:8). When you establish appetites as a family that are good, acceptable, and true, your children are more likely to manage their own appetites as they get older according to the values they learned in your home.

First, I would say pray and seek insight from God in regard to the plans He has for your family choices. I personally don't think there is a magical age to start giving certain freedoms to your children. Decide today if you haven't already what specific boundaries and standards you will have for your children. If you don't nail down your own convictions ahead of time, your children and their peer group will establish these instead of you.

If you haven't taken time to grapple over what you believe and why, the undercurrent of the culture will suck your family into a sea of conflicting and confusing values and compromises. This is particularly important with clothing, media choices, outside activities, and business. Your children are much less likely to question and push against you if your standards have been taught and explained ahead of time. And then ask yourself, am I being unreasonable with my teens? What are the issues to die over and what issues can I show grace?

When my son was a teen, I let him go without a belt on his jeans (something I could compromise on). I did not compromise on morality or on drinking or drugs, which were rampant with kids in our church. So choose your battlegrounds in the teen years well and hopefully your children will already have most of your values if you have laid a good foundation. Teen years are not easy because of all the voices and temptations. This is not a season in which to loosen up. Make your home the best place to be and you will settle some of your issues.

Question: I vacillate between being a dictator/police mom and feeling it is my duty to correct every sin and weakness and then wanting to be lenient and grace giving. What is the balance?

Our tendency as parents is to control our children. People (children) generally don't want to be controlled, and if you tell them what to do they will push away. Train and inspire them by building a foundation of love, grace, and investing lots of personal time in them.

I always said, "I cannot make you grow strong inside, I can only show you what I think is the best in life. But you must choose and exercise your own will toward excellence so that you can become strong inside and become the leader God made you to be!" These messages go far to produce in them beliefs that God will use them, that they have the ability and responsibility to be self-governed, and that they will become those who bring light to a dark world.

When children are never given choices and are told what to do, how to do it, when to do it, and are overmanaged and corrected, they never develop their own personal internal self- control. These kids are easy to spot in college when they go wild because they are no longer under the external control of their parents.

So strive to teach internal control to children by offering choices while walking alongside them and giving wise input and grace in regard to music, TV, books, and friend choices. God's heart toward us is that He is right there with us, but not controlling us. He says, "I will instruct you and teach you in the way you should go; I will counsel you with My eye upon you" (Psalm 32:8).

Question: *How do you break the habits you learned as a child? My family did a lot of negative and hurtful talk and nagging. To me it just natural, and I don't always know what is hurting my family and what is really helping.*

Understand that words are seeds planted into other people's lives. Many have experienced a similar home with negative, derogatory, and abusive talk. Words can have long-term effects, robbing us of our true identity if we choose to let them. All sinful habits are hard to break, but as a believer you are a new creation and God's grace is sufficient for you to overcome your past (2 Corinthians 12:9). Below is an acrostic to help remind me to use my words carefully.

W Words matter, given they are the most powerful way we can influence our children. With our words we are either building them up or tearing them down. "Let no unwholesome word proceed from your mouth, but only such a word as is good for edification according to the need of the moment, so that it will give grace to those who hear" (Ephesians 4:29). Stop and think, *Is what I am about to say going to benefit the listener?*

Proverbs 18:21 says, "Death and life are in the power

of the tongue, and those who love it will eat its fruit." Stop and think, *Am I bring life or death to the listener?*

O Owning up to your weakness is actually the first step in the right direction. We moms are going to blow it since we are humans. A mom who can acknowledge her own failings, apologize to those she's hurt, forgive herself, and then move on is a mom who models humility. Righting a wrong takes more than just saying "sorry"; It takes admitting what you did, voicing a sincere apology, asking anyone you've offended to forgive you, and making restitution, if necessary. This is really important to do with our children when we blow it with them. Stop and think, *Am I a good role model for the listener?*

R Retrain you mind. What you fill your mind with is usually what comes out. So be careful with your media choices (music, news, TV, etc.) and what friends you choose. "Finally, brethren, whatever is true, whatever is honorable, whatever is right, whatever is pure, whatever is lovely, whatever is of good repute, if there is any excellence and if there is anything worthy of praise, dwell on these things" (Philippians 4:8). Stop and think, *How is my thought life?*

D Daily we are on a journey and each day is a new beginning as His mercies are new every morning (Lamentation 3:23). Decide to live in the freedom you have been given as a new creation. Stop and think, *Am I living one day at a time?*

S Seek truth. Start with God's word daily. Your husband or a friend can offer insight. Even professional help could be beneficial. Having someone with whom you can be transparent and talk about the shame, hurt, and confusion you experienced as a child is helpful. I'm grateful for the blood of Jesus that cleanses us from all sin (1 John 1:7). Be determined to learn and grow. You will be a better woman, not a bitter one. Choose words that heal, bring life, and empower those in your life. Stop and think, *Do I believe God's truth can transform my life?*

Question: My biggest challenge is just getting the "must do" stuff done . . . not so much making home and kids a priority, because they are. It's just that there are so many of them—six under seven and half years! I just feel like I need to be supermom and can't do it all.

There is so much involved in caring for small children and keeping a home and it is so easy to get overwhelmed. Remember that this season isn't going to last forever. They will grow and be able to help more and you might forget how overwhelming this time feels. It's important to realize you might not have a perfect house in this time of your life and that is really okay. We have to adjust our expectations about what we are truly capable of sometimes.

Build rhythms into your day and week when you can rally and straighten the house, set the table, have devotions, work on school, eat, and clean up after meals. Stick to your planned rhythms and plans, and if you do not get everything finished in the time allotted, put that task into the file drawer of life and work on it the next day.

Before each day, determine to set your heart to meet your family's needs and not feel that your life is in so much chaos. Having times throughout the day when you gather together to sit and read or to have just ten minutes to pick up can really help too. And it will help your heart to know those moments are built into your routine.

God has not given us more to do than we can do, so sometimes we just need to realize limitations and determine the most essential things that really are required of a mom with young children. Sometimes I think the voices of this world make a mom think she is supposed to do more than a natural life with children would require.

When things are really busy, it might also take a bit of preparation in advance to keep things running smoothly. Things like writing out a meal plan to use for your grocery list, planning school for older children during the younger children's nap times, or sorting laundry together as a fun game when the rest of the day's work is done are some examples of how to prepare.

Also, look at the things you have to do each day and find ways that you can simplify. Too many outfits are going to require more work from you in the laundry room; simple dinners with just a few ingredients are going to be easier to prepare than something more elaborate. And don't be afraid to ask for help! Maybe there is a younger teenager in your community who could get some experience babysitting and helping you around the house one afternoon a week?

Question: How do you respond as a mom when you discipline your child and she responds with the words "I hate you!"?

It is so painful when this happens and so easy to become emotional or take it personally when your children whom you love so much respond to you this way. It might be a good idea to think for a moment about where they might have heard this kind of language and talking before, and determine if the way you are talking to them is modeling this in any way.

You can tell your child that she is never allowed to say these words in your family and that all the members of your family are commanded to love one another. Give your child some kind of consequences of what she must do if she chooses to say those words again. Teach the child that God commands children to honor their parents and that saying those words does not give honor and that is why she is not allowed to use them. Work as a family to establish boundaries in all of your words and hearts, so that none of you use this language.

When a child is this frustrated, it is also a sign that she is hurting. I would find time to spend with her alone and really hear her heart. Let her talk to you and share with you and ask God to give you wisdom to hear her.

Question: *I have three boys, eight, five, and one and a half, and I homeschool. During school time my littlest one walks around fussing for attention and it effects how I school the other two. I become easily aggravated and impatient, and I feel like I am not giving them my best. Any advice for moms with small children who are schooling older children would be helpful.*

This season is a juggling act, for sure, and you need to accept the fact that it always will be changing and each day will be filled with interruptions. Do not expect it to be static and you will not be as impatient. This is a home first, and homes have life and the swaying of days and growth and love.

It is a good idea to spend a tiny bit of time with each boy individually. Start with the youngest first while the other two are making beds, getting dressed, or folding clothes. Read to him, hug him, and talk to him about what he gets to do that morning while you are working with his brothers. Then have some special toys that he gets to play with that are only brought out during school time. I had bubbles and stickers and coloring books and treats that were for the younger ones when I needed time with the older ones. And I used nap times as well.

For boys under ten there should be limited "sit still" school time. There can be some math games and maybe a page of math numbers and simple daily grammar. After reading aloud while they play with blocks or Legos or color, they go outside. I knew the morning was successful when they were acting out the story we just read! Boys need to run and play and wiggle and make noise, so this should be a part of your plan. I had my wildest child run each morning before we would sit down and read. I would time him and say, "Wow, you are burning up the grass you are so fast." This helped him settle down for our read-aloud time.

Question: Is it ever too late to start over? I have a teenager, and I can see so much insecurity and flaws in him that I blame myself for. Is there any hope to make amends now, or is it too late?

Just like it is never too late for Christ to do a miracle in a person's life, it is never too late for Christ to change things around in the lives of our children. That is what Christ came for—to change lives and give second chances. We can work on the relationship now and enjoy the rest of our lives in a happier family.

Most of all, sweet mamas, take a deep breath. Children, family, and mothering are organic, natural realms of life. God designed them all because they were excellent designs and filled with potential for joy and deep belonging and fulfillment. Enjoy and know that God loves you, His child, and is on your team! He will bless you and show you His grace. And Sarah Mae and I are praying His blessing and grace for all of you who read this book!

Visit www.DesperateMom.com
for free resources, more encouragement, and help.

Find us on Facebook at
www.Facebook.com/DesperateBook.

Follow our conversation on Twitter by
searching for #DesperateMom.

A Special Note to Single Moms

I believe single moms are especially beloved by God. He is with you and will support you as you look to him and will work secretly in the hearts of your sweet children, because they, too, are beloved by him.

It is my prayer that many of you will find a mentor to love and support you in your challenging and unique calling, so that you will not have to walk this road alone. One of my very dear friends Pam Graves is a single mom who has modeled such faith, grace, and strength over the years and I asked her to share some of her thoughts about being a single mom.

—Sally

Because I grew up in a divorced home and knew first-hand the pain associated as a child from a single parent home, I did not plan on being divorced or becoming a single working mom of five children. Yet, when spiritual matters go unattended in one's life, patterns tend to repeat themselves.

I can honestly say my five children are "standing on my shoulders" and are shaking up the communities where they land, whether it be public school for the youngest three, college sports for my second born daughter, or my oldest daughter who is presently en route to Berlin to answer the call to missions.

My sweet nest climbed to my shoulders as I desperately cried out to the Lord to make me a change factor in our family heritage. I still hold fast to the promises of my Maker that he will complete the good work he began in both me and my children.

There are ongoing battles of depression, loneliness, exhaustion, and character shaping in both my own life and my children. As I give every concern to my Heavenly Father, and press into God in the hard places, he is ever so faithful to meet me and my family in the desperate places, giving grace and lovingkindness to each of us in unique ways that reflect his nature and character.

It can be so easy to allow our circumstances to define us: "single," "working mom," "divorced." Even worse, we can buy into the lie that the world judges us because of our circumstances. Whether you are single, divorced, or married, it is imperative to fight the enemy who tries to tear us down.

And we fight, like David, with the power of God's Word. God defines us as an inherent treasure that he loved to the point of death. It's the same way we feel about our children. We fight through every battle, insecurity, deception, and fear that they too may know not only how much we love them but also know the God of the universe is rooting for them.

Our kids are counting on us. I want to leave a lasting legacy of love and service

Acknowledgments

Those who have helped and inspired Sarah Mae:

Jesse, my husband, and the man who freed me to write and live out who God made me to be. Thank you for giving me the words I needed to keep going. I love you.

Mom, I love you. I understand so much more now, of who you are and of who I am. Thank you for being real.

Sally Clarkson, my mentor, friend, and advocate. You are grace to me. Thank you for being my adopted mama. You inspire me to be a wholehearted mother. And thank you for saying yes to writing this book!

Ginny Walls, thank you for helping me edit the first round of chapters for *Desperate*, and for being such an encouragement to me! I appreciate you so very much!

Lysa Terkeurst, thank you for seeing something in me and connecting me with those who could make publishing a book possible.

Esther Fedorkevich, thank you for believing in me and getting me publishing deals. You made it happen!

The Lititz Starbucks crew: Dave, Lynn, Valerie, Jocelyn, Zach, Ashley, Andy, Kristin, and everyone else there. You all serve the best salted mochas. Thank you for keeping me caffeinated while writing this book. You all rock.

Alice Rowan, my Starbucks buddy. You are a beautiful soul. Thank you for keeping me sane during my writing days. Keep stumbling by faith, my friend.

Angie Sollenberger, my helper and friend. Thank you for not judging my laundry piles or my messy bedroom. Thank you for playing with my babes, so I could write, and thank you for loving our family well. We love you and are thankful for you!

Erin Ulrich, you know why you're in here. Also, I think you are brilliant.

Susan Hoover, thank you for being the most normal mother-in-law I know! You are a godly example in my life and I am grateful for you. Love you.

Joel Miller, thank you for going to bat for our ideas. Appreciate you immensely.

My amazing blog readers. YOU all are the reason for this book! YOU all are the ones who believed in my words and encouraged me on. YOU all are my inspiration. Thank you over and over again for your friendship.

What a sweet blessing that you included me on this wonderful project, Sarah Mae. Thank you so much.

For you, my sweet Lord, for opening up the treasures of motherhood, I am most grateful.

I am so very honored for the countless, wonderful women who

read my books and blog and who attend our moms' conferences. Your encouragement is a blessing beyond expectation.

My precious friends who serve at every ministry event—you are indeed my angels from God.

To Joel, my son, who was the pillar of strength and the encouragement who helped us complete this book, my heartfelt thanks.

About the Authors

Sarah Mae is the wife of Jesse and the mother to three spunky, beautiful children. She is listed as one of the Christian Broadcasting Networks Six Women Leaders to Follow on Twitter and is an influential blogger, conference host, and author of the best-selling eBook *31 Days to Clean: Having a Martha House the Mary Way.*

Sarah Mae has established herself in social media by cultivating blogs and websites that have impacted thousands of women all over the world. She is the cofounder and cohost of Allume Social, a national Christian women's blogging conference, and is a contributing writer to the DaySpring blog incourage.me (a division of Hallmark).

Sarah Mae spends her days homemaking, home-educating, writing, reading, and drinking coffee.

Her family embraces life in the beautiful Amish countryside of Pennsylvania. You can connect with her at these places:

SARAHMAE.COM

WWW.FACEBOOK.COM/SARAHMAEWRITES

WWW.TWITTER.COM/SARAHMAE

Sally Clarkson is the mother of four wholehearted adult children. She is a popular conference speaker, and the author of numerous books and articles on Christian motherhood and parenting, including *The Mission of Motherhood*, *The Ministry of Motherhood*, *Seasons of a Mother's Heart*, *The Mom Walk*, *Dancing with My Father*, and *Educating the WholeHearted Child* (contributor). Her books have been translated into six languages.

Married to her best friend, Clay, for over 30 years, she ventured with him in ministry starting Whole Heart Ministries to encourage and equip Christian parents to raise wholehearted Christian children. Together, they write and publish books through Whole Heart Press, offer Mom's conferences for mothers, and minister online through several blogs and websites. Since 1998, Sally has ministered to thousands of mothers through her Mom Heart Conferences and Leader Intensive Training weekends and loves discipleship and mentoring other women. She has spoken across the U.S., and on four continents.

The Clarksons live in Monument, Colorado. Sally's children are her best friends and she loves strong Austrian coffee, English tea in real china, traveling, close friends, reading, music, bread-baking, and long walks in nature.

You can find Sally at:

Itakejoy.com—her personal blog
Momheart.org—a network of mom writers she created
Wholeheart.org –her ministry organization